TEXTILE
SEASCAPES

Alison Whateley

TEXTILE
SEASCAPES

✳ THE CROWOOD PRESS

CONTENTS

Introduction   7

1   Tools and Equipment   9
2   Finding Inspiration   17
3   Elements of Composition   31
4   Exploring Colour and Texture   41
5   Creating a Simple Small Seascape   49
6   Working on a Larger Scale   57
7   Creating a Semi-Abstract Seascape   65
8   Adding Hand Stitching and Mixed Media   71
9   Mounting and Framing   83
    Manufacturers and Suppliers   94

    Index   95

INTRODUCTION

Sewing has been a part of my life since my childhood. I first learned the skills of hand stitching before being taught how to use a sewing machine by my nan in my early teens. However, textile art using free-motion machine embroidery is something that I only discovered in my forties. I've always had a love of both fabric and stitch as well as a love of art, so the idea that I could create art with fabrics and draw with my sewing machine needle was something that immediately captured my imagination.

In this book, I focus on creating textile art seascapes. Living and working in Devon, I am fortunate enough to have two very different coastlines right on my doorstep offering an abundance of inspiration. The north coast is characterised by its wild beauty, with tall, rugged cliffs, spectacular views and long sandy beaches, whereas the south coast has many beautiful estuaries and small sandy coves.

It is said that some of our earliest and most vivid memories are made on visits to the seaside and, for many of us, these early experiences kindle an enduring love affair with the coast. That is certainly true for me, and nowadays the coast is where I go to relax and find freedom from the hustle and bustle of daily life. I enjoy whiling away a few hours with a bit of beach combing, or just spending some time sitting on the beach watching the waves roll in. Every time I visit the coast it is different. Not only does it change with the seasons and with the light, but also with the changing of the tides. I use the camera on my phone to record what I see and, once back at my studio, I use those photographs to inspire my work.

Creating seascapes with fabric and stitch doesn't have to be difficult, or complicated. Great results can be achieved with even the simplest of designs, so if you haven't done anything like this before, a simple design is where I suggest you start. This book covers everything you will need to know, from the equipment and materials you will use and how to get started with simple designs, through to the creation of more complex pieces and the development of your work over time as your skills evolve.

So, come with me on a journey into the world of textile art seascapes. I hope I can encourage you to have a go and that you will fall in love with creating them, just as I have.

OPPOSITE: Textile artwork depicting North Beach, Iona. (Photo: Southgate Studios)

CHAPTER 1

TOOLS AND EQUIPMENT

It's always exciting to start something new but, before you get stuck into creating your first textile art seascape, let's take a look at the basic tools and materials you will need to help you achieve results you will be proud of. If you are a seasoned stitcher then you will probably have most of the things you need already.

THE SEWING MACHINE

Of course, it is possible to create beautiful pieces of textile art without a sewing machine. Hand-stitched works such as tapestry have been created for centuries, and the best often find a place in major museums and art galleries. However, to create the style of work seen in this book, a sewing machine is an essential piece of equipment.

The first thing to point out regarding sewing machines is that you don't need an 'all-singing all-dancing' machine with hundreds of built-in stitches and computer control. A basic electric machine that is adaptable to free-motion machine embroidery will be perfectly adequate.

The only important requirement for your machine is that you will need some way of deactivating the feed dogs (the two rows of teeth underneath the presser foot that normally pull the fabric under the needle to help you stitch garment seams, for example, in a straight line). Deactivating the feed dogs gives you the ability to move the fabric in any direction you wish.

Most modern machines have a control that allows you to drop the feed dogs, although on some machines you will need to fit a plate that clips in place over the feed-dog teeth instead.

It is also important that your machine is maintained in good working order. I would recommend having it serviced every 12 months regardless of how much you use it, as a build-up of fibres and dust can soon cause problems

Work in progress on my sewing table. I am using variegated, hand-dyed scrim to build a grassy foreground.

OPPOSITE: Choosing the materials to create the foreground on a small seascape.

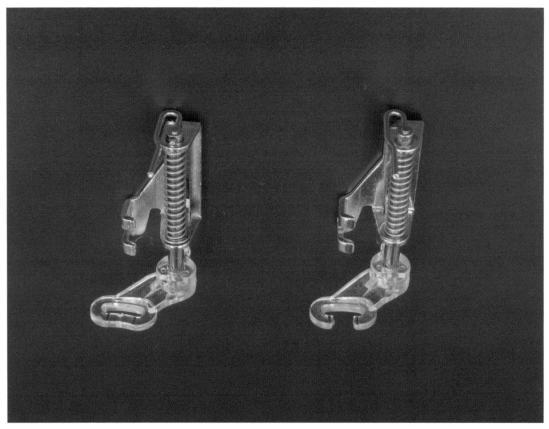

Free-motion/darning feet. You can clearly see the difference between the closed-toe design on the left, and the open-toe design on the right.

STEP-BY-STEP GUIDE TO SETTING UP YOUR SEWING MACHINE

1. Place your machine on a sturdy table with a comfortable working height, plug it in and switch it on.
2. Drop your feed-dog teeth. Please refer to your machine manual to find the switch to do this. Alternatively, if your machine has a plate to cover the feed-dog teeth then clip that in place now.
3. Attach your darning/free-motion foot.
4. Set your stitch length to zero, or as close to zero as your machine will permit. Some makes of machine only go down to 0.2, but that is absolutely fine.
5. Always start a new project with a new needle. I use a size 75/11 embroidery needle for the majority of the stitching I do – I will look at

needles and needle sizes in more detail later in this chapter.
6. Thread up your sewing machine as normal with your choice of top thread and bobbin thread.
7. Adjust the top tension on your machine to ensure that your bobbin thread is not visible on the top of your work when stitching. Top tension on most machines will usually be set between 4 and 3 for normal sewing, so you will usually need to reduce this for free-motion sewing. The exact setting will vary from one machine to another, though, so practise stitching on a scrap of fabric first to make sure you get the setting correct.
8. When you are happy that everything is set up correctly, you are now ready to start.

that, if left for any length of time, can result in expensive repairs.

You will also need a darning foot or free-motion foot. Most machines are not supplied with this foot as a standard accessory, but you can easily obtain one online or from your local sewing machine shop. It is important to get one which is compatible with your make of machine, so ask for some advice if you are not sure.

There are two styles of free-motion foot, 'open-toe' or 'closed-toe'. The open-toe foot is horseshoe-shaped and comes in metal or clear acrylic. The closed-toe foot is a completely closed ring, again available in either acrylic or metal.

For most machines, either type of foot will be available from your supplier, and which foot you choose comes down to personal preference. I find that an open-toe foot gives me greater visibility of my work and allows me to easily tuck threads out of the way before starting to sew. On the other hand, a closed-toe foot is useful if you are stitching over loose-weave fabric or loose threads, as they will not get tangled up in the foot as you stitch.

CUTTING TOOLS

Scissors

Although there are many different types of scissors for specific tasks, I find that I only use two different pairs regularly: a medium-sized pair of fabric scissors and a pair of embroidery scissors.

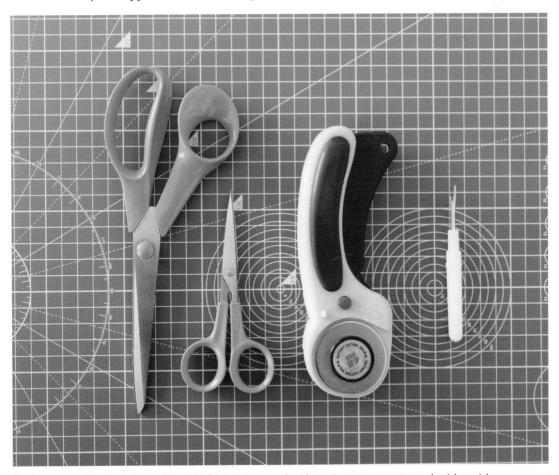

A selection of cutting tools: from left to right, fabric scissors, embroidery scissors, rotary cutter and quick-unpick.

Fabric scissors

It is really important to make sure that fabric scissors are kept in tip-top condition, so keep them solely for cutting fabric. That way they will cut easily and accurately. If you need to cut other materials such as paper, use a general-purpose pair instead of your fabric scissors.

Embroidery scissors

These are much smaller than fabric scissors and have long, fine tips that make them ideal for all your intricate and delicate cutting needs. Again, they should be kept for cutting fabric only.

Quick-unpick

Although unpicking free-motion machine embroidery is certainly a challenge – and something I would suggest you avoid if possible – a quick-unpick is still a useful tool to have in your sewing box.

Rotary cutter

A rotary cutter is a very useful tool for cutting straight lines in fabric when used in conjunction with a clear grid ruler and a self-healing cutting mat. Rotary cutting tools have a very sharp circular blade that is replaceable and can be retracted for safety. They are available in a range of sizes, usually with blade diameters of 60mm, 45mm, 28mm or 18mm. If you only want to purchase one, the 45mm size is the most useful. Clear grid rulers and self-healing cutting mats also come in a range of sizes and shapes.

CUTTING MAT

A cutting mat is essential to protect your work surface if you are going to use a rotary cutter. The most common type is self-healing; a self-healing surface not only makes the mat last longer but also reduces the blunting of blades.

These mats come in a variety of sizes and can be used in conjunction with a grid rule to obtain straight edges when cutting your fabric.

THREADS

Machine threads

There is a huge selection available, so choosing threads for free-motion machine embroidery can seem a little overwhelming. I would suggest choosing a quality brand. Although they may be a little more expensive, you will usually get a better finish to your work and your machine will run more smoothly.

Top thread

For most of my work, I use an invisible top thread, as I want to secure the fabric without leaving visible stitches. I use a clear polyester thread, but clear nylon thread is also available and is a cheaper alternative if you are just starting out.

I also use coloured threads from time to time, for example, if I want to add visible stitched detail that will enhance a piece of work. When it comes to coloured threads, I use polyester multipurpose threads as I prefer their matt finish. Alternatively, if you would like your stitching to have a shinier finish you can use embroidery threads. Which type of thread you choose is a personal preference and will to an extent depend on your individual style as an artist.

Bobbin thread

With the exception of invisible thread – which if used in the bobbin as well as on the top tends to jam up the machine – the bobbin thread can be the same thread you have used on the top.

However, bobbin-specific thread is also available, which is what I use myself. Bobbin-specific threads are fine, strong threads – usually made from polyester – that are less likely to break or show through on the top of your work (unless your machine settings are incorrect). They are also cheaper than top threads. I use white bobbin-specific thread with invisible or pale top threads and black bobbin-specific thread with darker top threads.

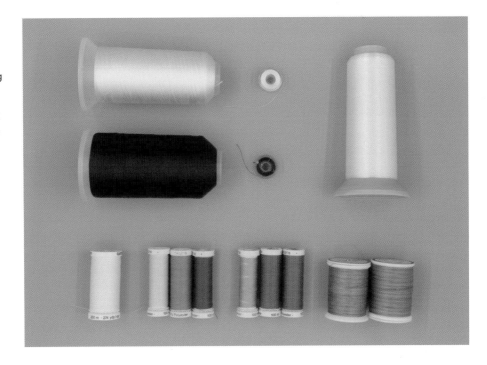

A selection of threads in suitable colours for creating seascapes; along with invisible thread and white and black bobbin threads.

Hand embroidery threads

I often use hand embroidery threads to add final stitched details to my work. These threads, which are six-stranded, come in a huge range of colours, but a small selection will be fine to start with.

NEEDLES

Machine needles

When buying needles for your sewing machine, always choose good-quality needles and change them regularly.

Machine needle sizes are defined by two numbers. One number is the European size, the other the American size. For example, a needle size of 75/11 represents a European size of 75 and an American size of 11. European sizes range from 60 to 120, while American sizes range from 8 to 19. For machine needles, the larger the size number, the thicker the needle.

In addition to size, machine needles are also categorised by type. I am not going to list every type of machine needle here, as that would need a separate chapter of its own. Instead, I will concentrate on those you will want to consider for creating your textile art:

- Universal needles range in size from 60/8 to 120/19. When I first started, I used standard universal needles for free-motion machine embroidery with very acceptable results. I would suggest using a size 80/12 if you choose to do this.
- Embroidery needles range in size from 75/11 to 90/14 and differ from universal needles in two ways:
  - To prevent breaking or fraying of your thread as the needle goes rapidly in and out through your fabric, the eye of an embroidery needle is made larger than that of a universal needle.
  - The 'scarf' of an embroidery needle – the indentation on the back of the needle that runs from the eye up the shaft – is specially designed to create less strain on your thread, which also results in less fraying and breakage.

- 'Metallic' needles come in size 80/12 and are designed specifically for use with metallic threads. They have a larger eye than an embroidery needle and come with a fine shaft and sharp point to prevent breakage and shredding of the thread. They are also ideal for use with monofilament thread (invisible nylon thread or invisible polyester thread).

Hand needles

These also come in a variety of sizes, so I would recommend choosing a good-quality multipack of needles that will stand you in good stead for all general hand-sewing needs.

Beading needles

These are much finer and more flexible than standard needles, allowing them to pass through the – often very narrow – threading holes in beads.

There are various types and sizes available, but I use English beading needles which are long, thin and flexible. They are available in a range of sizes from 10–15 (unlike machine needles, the larger the number the *finer* the needle), but I find that a size 10 is suitable for the majority of beading that I add to my work.

FABRICS

Backing fabrics

I use a fabric called Fine Firm Tarlatan Scrim as the backing for my work. This is an open-weave cotton fabric stiffened with starch; originally manufactured to be used in the printing industry for cleaning intaglio plates. I prefer not to use an embroidery ring when working as I find it too restrictive, so I needed to find a fabric that was fairly lightweight but firm enough without using a ring that it would not pucker up when stitching. For me, Fine Firm Tarlatan Scrim does the job perfectly.

One possible alternative material would be a lightweight calico, which is an unbleached, unfinished fabric made from cotton fibres. Although this is a popular choice, you will need a thicker fabric to get the same stiffness and even then, I find calico to be more prone to puckering.

Decorative fabrics

Decorative fabrics are those where you will use their colour and texture to create your piece of art. I would suggest collecting a selection of the following materials when starting to create textile seascapes:

It is a good idea to pull together a colourful selection of plain and patterned fabric scraps in coastal shades to give you inspiration before you begin.

- Lightweight fabrics such as cotton or poly-cotton (either plain or patterned).
- Loose-weave fabrics.
- Organza and fine nets.
- Lace.
- Mulberry bark (this is a specialist material which I use to represent waves, although white lace can be a good alternative).

Although some of your materials will need to be bought from new, I would also keep an eye out in charity shops and online marketplaces for suitable pieces to allow you to add to your stash gradually over time. Searching for second-hand fabrics can not only yield unusual patterns and textures but is kinder to both your pocket and the environment.

MISCELLANEOUS EQUIPMENT

Temporary fabric adhesives

Although some people prefer to use pins to hold their fabric pieces in place when stitching, I find that a temporary fabric adhesive works much better for my style. Available in spray or glue pen form, this temporarily holds your fabric in place while you stitch. I also find temporary adhesive useful as you can smooth the fabric out so that it doesn't wrinkle during sewing. I tend to use spray adhesive most of the time, with a glue pen reserved for fixing the tiniest of pieces. Please remember to follow the manufacturer's instructions regarding ventilation when using spray adhesive.

Erasable fabric pens

An erasable pen is extremely useful for drawing out your design directly onto the fabric, as it will not leave a permanent mark.

Heat-erasable pens are my preferred option as you can use your iron to remove the markings immediately. I also like the fact that they come with a fine 0.7mm nib, so it is much easier to draw detailed lines and know exactly where to stitch, even if the lines are close to one another.

Other alternatives are water-soluble and air-erasable pens. Water-soluble pen markings disappear when in contact with water, whereas air-erasable pen markings fade away naturally over a period of between two and seven days.

Pencils and paper for sketching your design

Although I don't sketch out my designs beforehand, this is only a personal preference: you may prefer to try out ideas on paper before you start choosing and cutting fabric. A sharp pencil in the range 2B to HB and plain white paper are ideal for this.

Steam iron and ironing board

Although specialist crafters' irons are available, a standard steam iron will be fine for pressing your work, as long as it is in good working order. Make sure that the base of your iron is completely clean before using it as you don't want to damage or mark your work.

If you are short of space, you can always use a tabletop ironing pad instead of an ironing board.

A working 'matt' (or mount)

This is a piece of mount board with a window (aperture) cut out of it in the dimensions that you want your finished piece to be. Many people will refer to this as a mount, but the correct term is a matt – so that is the word I will use throughout this book.

I have standard sizes I prefer to work with regularly, and I keep 'working matts' in those dimensions at my studio so that they are always available. Alternatively, you could cut a window in the size you require out of a piece of card or thick paper or use the matt from an existing frame if you already have one.

I find being able to offer up a matt over my piece of work periodically as I create it is enormously useful, as it helps me to see how the finished piece will look.

CHAPTER 2

FINDING INSPIRATION

nspiration for creating art is all around us, even if we don't always notice it. So, when looking for inspiration for your textile art seascapes, be sure to gather material from numerous sources as this will help you to develop your ideas. If you have a dedicated sewing room you may wish to create a mood board of ideas that you can refer to; alternatively, you can keep all your ideas in a notebook or scrapbook.

VISITING THE COAST

The coast has been a source of inspiration for artists throughout history. The rhythmic ebb and flow of the tides, the vast expanse of the horizon where the sea meets the sky, and the ever-changing colours and textures of the shoreline all serve as a captivating canvas for creative expression. Whether it's the tranquillity of a calm beach at dawn or the dramatic intensity of a stormy seascape, the coast offers an inexhaustible source of material for your coastal art.

If you are able to visit the coast – whether to walk the dog on the beach every day or just to visit from time to time for a holiday – make sure you go armed with a way of recording what you see. I prefer to take photographs; these days the camera on a mobile phone is more than adequate for this purpose. Alternatively, you could take a sketchbook and pencil, or even a few paints if you wish, and while away an hour or two sketching and enjoying the sea air. Whatever method you choose, the main thing is that you create a record that you can refer back to later.

The coastline is ever-changing, so there will always be new things to discover. The view will look completely different at high tide, for example, compared to when the tide is out, and if you visit after a storm, you will find plenty of washed-up flotsam and jetsam that you can not only photograph or sketch for future reference but also collect – where permitted – to incorporate into your work (*see* Chapter 8 on adding mixed media).

Inspiration comes in many forms, so think about recording the colours that you observe as well as the things you see. I photograph colour combinations in rock forms, seaweed and pebbles, and also record close-ups of the colours of old fishing ropes and wooden boats. You don't have to include these items in your seascapes unless you want to – just using some of their colour combinations will give your work an authentic coastal feel.

OPPOSITE: Textile artwork depicting Widemouth Bay on the North Cornish Coast. (Photo: Southgate Studios)

Widemouth Bay on the North Cornish coast, where waves and the incoming tide acted against each other to create patterns and shapes on the beach.

Fishing equipment stored on the beach can suggest other colours and textures for you to use in your work.

Inspirational colour combinations can often be revealed by the erosion of coastal rocks.

I also regularly photograph waves. Each one that rolls in is different from the last, and as well as observing and recording how individual each one is, the activity of wave-watching can be very relaxing and meditative. So, whether you're sketching, photographing or collecting, if you can get out to the coast make sure to record the small details as well as the bigger picture.

A windy day gives you the opportunity to capture the shape of waves rolling onto the beach, as well as showing a more subtle range of colours.

MAGAZINES

Magazines are great resources that should definitely be utilised. We all love to browse through a magazine, whether over a coffee, on the daily commute, or in the doctor's waiting room, so look out for anything coastal that inspires you, whether that be the subject matter, the composition or the colours. Some magazines are coastal-themed or have regular articles on coastal living; these would be an ideal place to start.

As you browse magazines, you can cut out or photocopy any images that catch your eye. I would suggest keeping them in a physical scrapbook or a digital inspiration journal so that they are easily accessible when you need them. Of course, if you have picked up a magazine to read from a public place then this may not be possible, in which case take a photo of it on your phone camera and save that to a folder of ideas.

BOOKS

Finding inspiration for your textile art seascapes in books can be a wonderful way to explore different perspectives and artistic interpretations of the sea. Books offer a wealth of imagery and ideas that can inspire you. You may already have books at home that you can refer to, but if you don't then your local library is a great resource. I would suggest starting in the nonfiction section.

Travel and photography books that feature coastal regions, beaches and seaside landscapes are particularly good. These books capture the unique atmospheres and moods of different coastal locations around the world.

FINDING INSPIRATION ONLINE

In today's digital age, the internet's boundless wealth of resources makes finding inspiration for your textile art so much easier. There is a huge amount of material available online to help, not only with composition but also technique, all of it available on demand, 24 hours a day.

Visual social media platforms such as Instagram or Pinterest provide a constant stream of subject matter, and I would definitely recommend exploring them to see what you can find.

Instagram

Instagram is primarily a visual platform, frequented by many artists and creators as a place they can showcase their work, so it is the perfect place to look for ideas for your seascapes. Begin by searching for popular coastal and beach-related hashtags like #CoastalArt, #Seascape, #BeachArt, #beachphotography and #OceanInspiration. These hashtags will lead you to a wide range of coastal-themed artwork. I regularly use many of these hashtags myself when posting my own coastal-inspired art. Instagram allows you to save posts privately, so when you come across something that resonates with you, save it to your personal collection for future reference and inspiration.

It is also worth trying out Instagram's Explore feature which suggests posts and accounts based on your interests. Simply click on the magnifying glass icon to explore content tailored to your preferences.

Pinterest

Pinterest is a fantastic platform for finding inspiration. It's rich in images, ideas and curated boards that cater to every subject you can imagine. To discover inspiration for your coastal art on Pinterest, consider using specific search terms in the Pinterest search bar to refine your results. Begin with keywords like 'coastal art',

'seascapes', 'beach photography' or 'ocean-inspired art' to find relevant pins. When you find a pin that resonates with you, click on it to view more details, and explore related pins. Pinterest's recommendation system will lead you to a vast array of coastal artwork and ideas. Also, look for users who curate boards dedicated to coastal and beach-themed art. By following these boards, you'll have a continuous stream of coastal art appearing in your Pinterest feed.

When you discover an image you like, you can use Pinterest's visual search feature to discover more pins with similar themes or colour palettes. Simply click on an image, then click the magnifying glass icon.

Finally, you can create mood boards of your own to organise your finds, which allows you to locate them again easily at a later date.

Free stock images

I would also suggest taking a look at free stock image websites, as you can access a vast array of coastal scenes and elements on these, to inspire and inform your textile art. The images can serve as a valuable starting point, helping you visualise and bring your coastal art ideas to life.

Reputable websites such as pmp-art.com and Unsplash offer high-quality, copyright-free images of coastal scenes, beaches, seascapes and more.

When searching for images, narrow down your search by using specific keywords like 'ocean horizon', 'beach waves' or 'coastal views'. You can save images that capture your imagination on Pinterest.

Always review the licensing terms of the stock images you use. While many free stock image websites offer images for creative use, especially those using so-called 'creative commons' or 'copyleft' licensing, it's still essential to respect copyright and attribute the content creators when required.

LOOKING AT OTHER ARTISTS' WORK

Another really good place to look for ideas is the work of other artists – and not just textile artists. Look at artists using other media who create coastal works. What sort of views do they create? What style have they got? What colours do they use? If they paint, how do they use their brush strokes to represent the scene, and how could you recreate something similar in fabric and stitch? This will help you to think about how you represent various elements in your own work.

However, while it's perfectly acceptable to draw inspiration from other artists, make sure your work remains original and reflects your own creative voice. If you decide to share your work on social media, for example, make sure you credit the artist that was the source of your inspiration. You can use phrases such as 'inspired by' or 'in the style of'. Most social media platforms also have features for tagging and crediting other users. Remember that giving credit to the artist is not just about legal obligations but also about fostering a supportive and respectful creative community.

Remember, you don't have to limit yourself to using just one image as your inspiration for your work. I will often work with multiple images, pulling elements from each to build my own unique piece. I use images as a foundation for my creative expression, adding my own artistic perspective and style as I progress.

SOURCING MATERIALS THAT INSPIRE YOU

Sourcing materials that inspire your textile art is a crucial aspect of the creative process. Finding the right fabrics, embellishments and other components for your seascapes will make a huge difference when it comes to how you view the finished piece. Generally, when creating seascape and coastal-inspired art, most people will work principally in a colour palette of blues, greens and sandy browns. But that is not to say that you can't include small amounts of other colours too, so having a range of fabric colours is essential. Below are a few ideas of where to source your materials.

* Traditional fabric shops are excellent places to start to acquire materials. Explore their wide selection of textiles, from basic cotton fabrics and silks to speciality materials such as organza, net or linen. Touch, feel and inspect different fabrics to discover variations in texture as well as colours that resonate with you. You will often only need small quantities so you should always check out the shop's remnants section for any bargains.

* There are a large number of online fabric retailers that offer an extensive range of materials. You can search for specific fabrics, or browse through categories to find unique and inspiring textiles that may not be readily available in local stores. But a note of caution: I personally buy very few fabrics online, as it can be very difficult to determine the true weight, texture and colour of textiles from what you see on the screen. I have been caught out several times when what I received was not really what I was expecting, particularly concerning colour.

It's surprising what useful materials you can find in charity shops. Here you can see a collection including an old shirt, some ladies' scarves, bedsheets and some fabric remnants.

It's easy to be overwhelmed with choices at a craft store, so try to be selective. Here I have gathered a range of embroidery threads, ribbons, sequins, beads and wax cords in coastal colours that work well together.

- Charity shops are treasure troves for sourcing materials that inspire creativity. Look at clothing, ladies' scarves, bed linens, and embellishments such as lace and buttons that you can repurpose into your textile art. The combination of textures, colours and patterns can be highly inspiring, and I love to use these things in my work. This eco-friendly approach can be both environmentally responsible and artistically rewarding, as well as providing much-needed funds for a charity.
- Craft stores offer a wide range of embellishments and materials that can enhance your textile art. Beads, sequins, ribbons and speciality threads can provide inspiration for adding intricate details and texture to your work.
- Don't forget to delve into your own collection of materials, fabrics and textiles as well. You will sometimes find materials that you have collected over time and then forgotten about, that might be just what you need.

A LOOK AT HOW FINISHED PIECES OF ART REFLECT THEIR SOURCES OF INSPIRATION

Let's take a look at two of my coastal works to see where my initial inspiration came from, how I created my own representation of these images, and how the final pieces compare to the original scene. For both these pieces my inspiration came from photographs I took myself.

The key to using photographs as inspiration in art is determining what to incorporate in your work and what to leave out. This decision will hinge somewhat on the scale – and hence the appropriate level of detail – of your intended finished artwork. It's crucial to keep in mind that your creation will be *your* interpretation of the scene observed.

You possess the artistic freedom to simplify, reposition, insert and exclude elements. There's no need to depict every single tree on a headland or every individual pebble on a beach. In fact, attempting to do so would lead to an overly intricate piece, complicating the composition, confusing the viewer and potentially diminishing your satisfaction with your artistic endeavour.

The Exe Estuary, Dawlish Warren

For this piece, I have used a photograph I took while out walking on Dawlish Warren, close to the mouth of the River Exe in Devon.

I was immediately drawn to this image because it is of a place not far from my home, that I love to visit. The feelings of peace and tranquillity in the photograph were what I sought to convey when creating this artwork. I also liked the overall composition of the photo and admired the sense of depth it conveyed.

The piece of art I created measures 43cm × 23cm and largely mirrors the photo using fabric and stitching techniques – albeit with a touch of artistic interpretation. In the background, the hills adorned with trees were simplified into two pieces of fabric, aligning with the photo's softer distant view. This approach enhances a sense of depth by not overwhelming the viewer with minute detail.

I opted to streamline the depiction of the shoreline buildings, choosing to include just the three main houses, while still retaining the essence of the place. Similarly, when representing the groynes, I have not attempted to show each one that you can see in the photo. Instead, I have created my own representation of them.

For the stony area in front of the groynes, depicting every individual pebble, shell and piece of driftwood visible in the photograph would have been impossible. Therefore, I used various weights of lace and a few vintage

The Exe Estuary, Dawlish Warren, photographed at low tide. Note the sense of depth created by the softness of the distant hills and the detail in the foreground.

Here you can see the finished piece inspired by my photograph of the Exe Estuary. (Photo: Southgate Studios)

buttons to give an impression of the detail. This is much more pleasing to the eye and still adds texture and interest to the piece.

When you look at the completed artwork you can see how closely it compares to the original photograph.

Small headland view, North Devon
This photograph is of a completely different view, taken on the North Devon coast, looking out to sea. At first glance, you could be forgiven for thinking this image had much less detail in it

and was therefore much easier to represent, but that wasn't the case.

Deciding to create quite a small representation of this view, measuring just 12cm square, really added to the challenge. The principal impression I wanted to convey was the feeling of height from which the photo was taken, standing on the cliff edge looking down to the sea below.

When looking at my final piece you will see that the overall composition is pretty similar – although as the photograph itself is rectangular

A cliff-top view along the north Devon coast near Hartland Point. (Photo: Alison Whateley)

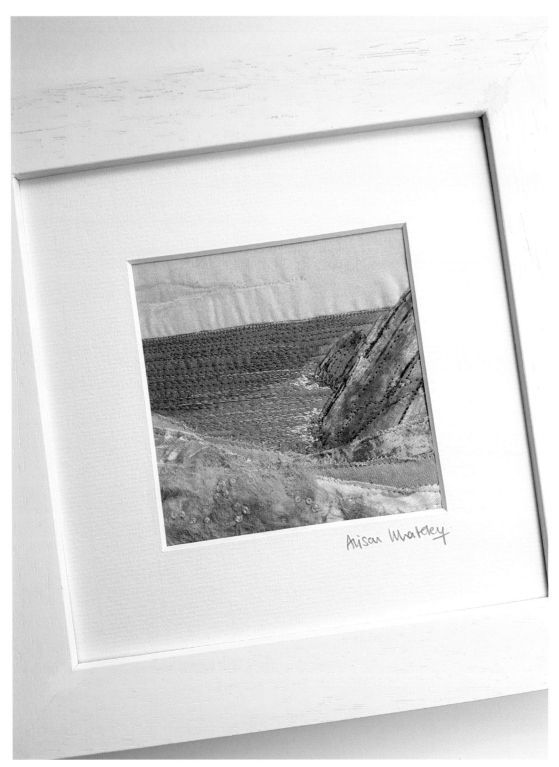

Finished piece inspired by the photograph taken near Hartland Point. (Photo: Alison Whateley)

and my piece is square, I did have to adjust what I included. Even though the piece was going to be small I still wanted to capture the ruggedness of the cliffs, with all their little nooks and crannies. I tried for some time to create this with fabric and stitch, but my initial attempts either looked overworked or felt flat, so a radical rethink was needed. In the end, I experimented with some pieces of dried tree bark – set at the correct angle they gave me just the effect I was looking for.

The grassy headland could have been represented with just a single piece of patterned or plain fabric, but I wanted to capture the texture of the rough scrub and the undulation of the ground while also creating foreground interest to enhance the composition and create a sense of depth. I used a combination of patterned and plain fabric to achieve this, cut at angles and overlaid with loose-weave green scrim that I manipulated before stitching in place. Adding a few bright yellow French knots then evoked the yellow colour of some of the grasses in the photo. The waves hitting the rocks were represented with free-motion machine stitching using a white polyester thread. I often use bleached mulberry bark to represent waves in my seascapes, but for a piece this small that wouldn't have worked because of the tiny area of the picture the waves occupy.

So, to sum up: a finished artwork is a result of the artist's journey from inspiration to creation. It should mirror both external influences and the individual artist's internal process, creating a unique expression of their vision and creativity. This interaction between inspiration and interpretation gives each artwork a sense of personal style.

CHAPTER 3

ELEMENTS OF COMPOSITION

Most books on art techniques focus on the methods for a specific medium (in this case textiles), and often assume a prior knowledge of composition on the part of readers. Many artists will claim that you either understand composition naturally or you do not, and that composition cannot be taught. This is true to an extent; some people do find it easier than others to create a pleasing composition. However, I also believe that the ability to produce good composition in your art can be developed. The key, I think, is to be constantly critical of your own work and strive to improve.

You may well have come across so-called 'rules of composition'; in my experience, these are more useful as a method of developing a discerning eye – which in turn will enable you to develop your own sense of composition – than they are as a formula to use in designing your own pieces.

In my workshops I will often need to help people with composition, suggesting changes in the placement of picture elements and letting them see the difference such a change makes. However, such immediate feedback is not possible in a book, so instead I will look at the various 'rules' and discuss how they might help you.

The word 'composition' refers to the harmonious arrangement of the parts of a work of art in relation to each other and to the whole. However, as well as simply the arrangement of parts, I will also look at other elements of composition you will need to consider in producing your art.

There have been many thousands of words written in those books that do specialise in composition – both for art in general and for photography – and I can do little more here than provide you with some initial guidelines.

FORM AND THE PLACEMENT OF ELEMENTS

The form of a piece describes the physical placement of the picture elements within the work, in relation to the edges. Not surprisingly, the shape and size you choose for your work can therefore have a significant impact on the feel of a piece of art and how you arrange your composition, which is one of the reasons that I always work with a sizing matt (or mount). Offering a matt up to the piece you're working on at intervals can dramatically improve your perception of how the finished piece will work and assist in all other aspects of composition.

Of course, the aperture in a matt can be any shape that it is possible to cut. However, whilst circular, elliptical and even irregular mounts have been used occasionally by artists, I will restrict this discussion to square or rectangular matts.

OPPOSITE: A photograph taken at Widemouth Bay shows a strong sense of depth due to linear and atmospheric perspective.

The first point to consider is the relationship between the lengths of the horizontal and vertical sides of the piece, known as the 'aspect ratio'. Square pieces can work well for some subjects as they offer a sense of symmetry and neutrality. Many subjects, though, will sit uncomfortably within the square because a square naturally leads your eye to the centre, which can unbalance the image.

Rectangular artworks clearly have more options available to explore in the construction of a pleasing composition. Firstly, there is the obvious distinction between a vertical or 'portrait' format, and a horizontal 'landscape' format. Despite the names, both horizontal and vertical formats are equally valid for landscapes or seascapes. A horizontal format is somewhat better for representing the width of a scene and is closer to the view seen by the human eye. A vertical format tends towards abstraction – almost like a vertical 'slice' of a landscape or seascape – and emphasises a sense of depth. The narrower the piece, the more extreme the abstraction.

Irrespective of the aspect ratio, the overall size of a piece can also have a significant impact on how you structure it. The use of textiles as an artistic medium places a constraint on the level of detail you can incorporate into a piece (although hand stitching can allow you to add fine detail where required). What this means is that creating a small piece will necessarily result in a simplified composition if it is not to look overworked and busy. Smaller pieces will also often be viewed in their entirety, whereas a larger piece, especially if viewed from close to, will only be understood by scanning the eye between places of interest.

Once we have decided on the shape and size of a piece, the next task in forming a pleasing composition is to consider the placement of elements within the frame. The objectives here are to produce both tension and balance, and to create a sense of movement. One of the advantages of textiles over pigment-based media – such as paint, pastel and ink – is that the elements of the composition can be easily repositioned, replaced or even removed as you assess the effect on the overall composition.

There is insufficient room in a book of this size to provide an exhaustive guide to the 'theory' of composition, and it wouldn't really be helpful anyway. As stated above, most artists use the theoretical principles of composition merely as a general guide. However, it can be useful to look at a few specific examples so that you can learn to think about composition in your own work.

I am going to show you how I have analysed two of my seascape pictures. The first, called *Morning Haze*, is a square piece, around 30cm × 30cm. As you can see, this is a calm piece, depicting a misty beach scene. The sense of calm is enhanced by the square composition, but there is still a sense of movement in the piece due to the placement of the elements.

In most nations, certainly those in Europe; North and South America; and some parts of Asia, our written language proceeds from left to right and from top to bottom of the page. For this reason, we tend to view pictures in the same way. In the case of *Morning Haze*, our eyes have a tendency to fix first on the distant headland on the left, then travel down to the debris on the beach on the right. After that they seek balance by travelling back across the beach to the other debris on the left, and then back up to the headland.

This creates a sense of movement and interest in the piece, but it also creates an implied triangle, which is one of the most effective compositional shapes in art. Triangular compositions are often seen in paintings dating as far back as the Renaissance masters.

Many other compositional ideas can be used but my advice would be to avoid trying to produce a piece that fits a formula. It's much better to produce a piece that you like and then analyse the piece afterwards to see how it works in terms of shape, eye lines and picture planes.

My picture *Morning Haze* is based on a misty morning on the beach. (Photo: Southgate Studios)

This is the route to developing an artistic eye. There are many books on composition available. The most accessible will be those books relating to composition in photography, many of which are available from public libraries. I would also suggest visiting art galleries if you have one nearby, and thinking about the way composition works in each piece you like. In particular, think about the way a composition causes your eyes to move around the image.

One other specific concept that you will find useful, however, is known as the 'rule of thirds'. The idea is that you imagine lines roughly dividing a picture into thirds, both horizontally and vertically. The points where those lines intersect are good places to position important parts of your composition, as they tend to attract the eye. The placement does not have to be exact, in fact, deviation from the exact thirds adds interest.

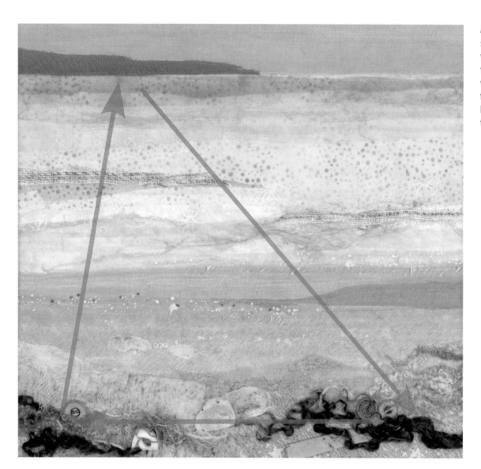

Morning Haze, showing the way a Western viewer's eye lines will move around from the top left to interpret the picture.

Morning Haze. The lines of travel of the viewer's eyes in the previous picture produce a triangle, one of the most common compositional forms in art as far back as the Renaissance.

The second example of one of my works, entitled *Solo*, depicts a sailboat on the River Exe. You can see that the placement of the boat is near to the lower-left intersection of the horizontal and vertical thirds lines. Note also that the opposite bank of the river, just visible through the mist, lies almost exactly at one-third of the height of the image.

The rule of thirds works to produce interest in a piece because of the natural tendency of the eye to seek balance. If you place a key object off-centre, then your eye will naturally travel back and forth between the object, and a point of balance on the other side of the picture. Sometimes there will be another object to provide balance. In the case of my piece *Solo*, the point of balance is in the misty sky, so the eye visualises a virtual point of balance even though there is nothing actually there. A more extreme off-centre position than one-third can be quite unsettling, so you will need to experiment to see what proportion produces

My picture *Solo*. A subtle, surprisingly complex composition in soft greys and blues. (Photo: Southgate Studios)

Solo, showing the placement of the boat and the far shoreline. These points approximate the positions using the rule of thirds.

Solo. The eye seeks balance for an off-centre subject, even if there is nothing there. The implied counterpoint (shown as an orange blur) creates movement in a piece.

the aesthetic effect that works the best for a particular composition. In the case of *Solo*, the position, the emptiness of the rest of the scene and the direction of travel of the boat out of the frame all combine to create a sense of solitude and journey towards home.

COLOUR

Colour is another important aspect of composition. In general, I usually choose a coherent colour palette for my pieces, even if this means I have to choose colours for objects that are different from their natural appearance; this is covered in depth in the next chapter.

In terms of composition, you should also think about the relative brightness of the colours you select. Balancing different colours will require your brighter colours to occupy a smaller area of your piece than more muted colours. So a monochrome seascape consisting of different shades of blue can frequently be enlivened by the addition of, say, orange; but, depending on placement, the area of orange will need to be small to avoid unbalancing the picture. Again, many more examples will be found in books on composition.

DEPTH

Finally, we will look at how to create a sense of depth in your picture. Seascapes rarely include linear elements that converge to a vanishing point, although man-made structures such as groynes and some rock formations do.

The same principles of reducing dimensions as things get further away also apply to the scale of individual things you include. Put simply,

Linear rock formations at Widemouth Bay on the North Cornish coast clearly show the way lines converge with distance.

Rocks on the beach at Widemouth Bay appear to get smaller as they get more distant, adding to the effect of depth.
(Photo: Alison Whateley)

elements at the front of your piece should be larger than those at the back, even if they are the same size in real life. That is easy when it comes to stones or vegetation at the very front, and cliffs or a headland on the horizon, but you should take special care to correctly size objects in the middle ground. We have all seen children's pictures where Mum and Dad are standing on the very edge of the sea and would be, if the perspective were correct, 20 feet tall. For that matter, a true-to-scale lighthouse placed on that distant headland in the picture *Morning Haze* would realistically be little more than a tiny grey smudge. Historically, even the great European painters of the early Renaissance struggled with perspective, often painting what they 'knew' to be there, rather than what they actually saw. You can clearly see the effect

on depth that the reducing scale of stones on a beach creates in this photograph taken in Cornwall.

As well as scale, you can also use the way colour changes with distance to show depth. Objects that are further away will exhibit a loss in colour saturation (this is called atmospheric perspective), especially when the atmosphere is less than clear due to dust, smoke or moisture. A distant headland will appear grey in real life, and the use of grey fabric and reduced detail can create the impression of distance. This photograph, taken at Widemouth Bay on the North Cornish Coast, clearly shows the effect of spray from the sea in muting the colour and reducing the contrast of the distant headlands compared to the foreground, so creating a sense of depth.

Heavy spray caused by a strong onshore wind causes the colours in the distant headlands to become desaturated, adding to the sense of distance.

CHAPTER 4

EXPLORING COLOUR AND TEXTURE

Fabric in textile art is more than just the canvas on which we place colours; it's a fundamental part of the creative process, like the paint on an artist's palette itself. Each fabric has its own unique qualities in terms of weight, weave, composition and colour. By choosing different fabrics, you can add depth, texture and character to your artwork. The fabric serves as both the foundation and the medium for textile art, allowing you to express your creativity and bring your artistic visions to life.

CHOOSING A COLOUR PALETTE

It is really worth taking your time when selecting a colour palette for a piece. The colours chosen will play a crucial role in conveying mood and atmosphere, so it is important to get it right.

I usually begin by collecting a selection of materials in colours and shades that I feel work well together, and that represent the intended composition. I often end up not using them all, but the initial selection provides a starting point to get the creative juices flowing. Generally, for seascapes, you will be looking for blues, greens and sandy tones which will form the foundation, but don't shy away from introducing complementary colours as well

(*see* the next section, 'Colour Theory and the Colour Wheel').

It is easy to be very literal in your approach to choosing colours – particularly if you are working from a photograph. The beauty of using fabrics instead of other media such as paint is that you can choose to incorporate both patterned and plain fabrics. In fact, I would encourage you to do this as, in my view, it enhances the overall appeal and interest of the final piece. Also, try experimenting with different shades and tones to create depth and dimension. As I progress through the process of creation I will frequently source additional materials to add to my initial selection; just make sure that what you add works with what has already been selected.

I have, on occasion, limited myself to just one colour and created a piece solely, for example, in shades of blue. This is known as a monochromatic palette.

Using this technique allows you to focus on other aspects of your artwork, such as texture, shape and composition, instead of colour. It's also quite a fun exercise.

The other important factor in pulling together a coherent palette is to consider the 'undertone' of a colour. For example, all colours can have either a warm or a cool undertone. Reds can be a blueish red (cool) or orangey red (warm). Blues can be greenish or tend more towards purple.

OPPOSITE: A textile artwork depicting the beach at the mouth of the River Otter at Budleigh Salterton in Devon. (Photo: Southgate Studios)

Seascape created in a calming blue monochromatic palette.

A selection of blue fabrics showing a greenish undertone to the blue.

A selection of blue fabrics showing a mid-blue undertone to the blue.

COLOUR THEORY AND THE COLOUR WHEEL

The colour wheel is a valuable tool for choosing colour combinations that are visually appealing and harmonious. It will help you create balance and unity in your work by understanding how different colours interact and influence each other.

The introduction of computing has resulted in several different colour models, such as red-green-blue for screens and cyan-magenta-yellow-black for printers, but we are concerned here with the earliest model, based on mixing of paint by artists.

It's based on the principles of colour theory and consists of three primary colours (red, blue and yellow), three secondary colours (green, orange and purple) and six tertiary colours, resulting in a total of 12 colours arranged in a circle.

Here's how the colour wheel works:

1. **Primary colours:** The foundations of the colour wheel are the three primary colours: red, blue and yellow. These colours are considered fundamental because they cannot be created by mixing other pigments together.

2. **Secondary colours:** Situated between the primary colours are the secondary colours, which are created by mixing equal parts of two adjacent primary colours. These secondary colours are green (from mixing yellow and blue), orange (from mixing red and yellow) and purple (from mixing red and blue).

3. **Tertiary colours:** Tertiary colours come next, found between the primary and secondary colours. They are created by mixing a primary colour with a neighbouring secondary colour. Examples of tertiary colours include red-orange, yellow-green and blue-purple.

4. **Complementary colours:** Complementary colours are opposite each other on the colour wheel. When placed next to one another, complementary colours create strong visual contrast and can make each other appear more vibrant. For example, red and green, blue and orange, and yellow and purple are complementary pairs.

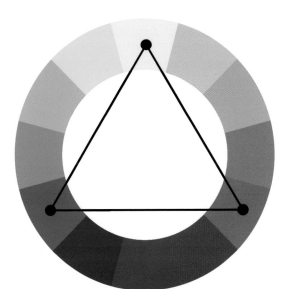

Red-Blue-Yellow colour wheel, indicating the three primary colours.

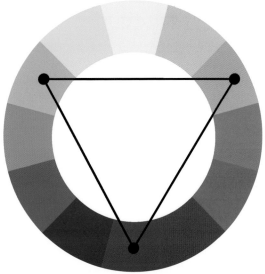

Red-Blue-Yellow colour wheel, indicating the three secondary colours; purple, green and orange.

5. **Analogous colours:** Analogous colours are situated next to each other on the colour wheel. They share a common primary colour and create a harmonious and cohesive colour scheme. For instance, red, red-orange and orange are analogous colours.

6. **Warm and cool colours:** The colour wheel can be divided into warm and cool colours. Warm colours (like red, orange and yellow) are associated with warmth, energy and vibrancy, while cool colours (like blue, green and purple) evoke a sense of calm, serenity and coolness.

SELECTING FABRICS BY WEIGHT AND TEXTURE

It's also important to choose weights and textures of fabric based on how they are going to be used in your picture.

As a general rule, I find it's good practice to opt for lightweight fabrics for distant elements while reserving thicker, more textured fabrics for the foreground.

You need to consider how the fabrics will sit once stitched and what effect you are trying to achieve. If, for instance, you are overlapping strips of fabric to create the sea in the distance of your piece, you don't want those fabrics to be too thick because once you have stitched them in place you will be left with visible ridges, which will look unnatural and draw the eye. So, instead, use lightweight fabrics like cotton or polyester cotton that when overlapped and stitched in place, just seamlessly blend into one.

Remember, too, that everything has to work together, so fabric weight has to be considered in conjunction with the size of the piece you are working on. If you are creating a small seascape you will not want to be using extremely thick fabrics in the foreground as they will be difficult to work with. It is hard enough to cut really small shapes from heavy fabrics, but once you try to stitch them in place you will find that the weave disintegrates. Reserve the heaviest fabrics for large pieces where you can really go to town.

SHEER FABRICS AND HOW TO USE THEM TO ACHIEVE A PAINTERLY FEEL

When people view my work, they often make comments such as: 'Oh I didn't realise it was fabric!' or 'I thought it was a painting!'. I take this as a great compliment, as that effect is what I am trying to achieve with my representational work. Right from the start of my artistic journey, I was interested in how I could use fabrics to achieve the feel of a painting, and after much experimentation, I developed the use of sheer fabrics to achieve this. The transparency and delicate nature of sheer fabrics result in the creation of beautiful, ethereal effects that can really take your work to another level.

I use many different sheer fabrics in my work but when I am looking at shading the sky and blending the sea, my favourites are organza and fine net.

Organza

Organza was traditionally made from silk, but nowadays the majority of organza is made from synthetic fibres, primarily polyester and nylon. Synthetic organza is cheaper than silk but can be prone to fraying. I don't tend to worry too much about whether it's silk or synthetic, instead concentrating on getting the correct shades I need.

Whether it's silk or synthetic, there are many different finishes of organza but below I have listed the ones that I use and the differences between them:

- **Crystal organza**. This is the most common and popular type of organza. It is soft, lightweight and has a subtle sheen. It can be made from silk or synthetic fibres.
- **Mirror organza**. This is typically made from polyester and is the shiniest form of organza.
- **Satin organza**. This boasts the shiny quality of satin, while still maintaining the crisp drape of organza.
- **Shot organza**. This refers to a type of organza fabric that has a two-tone or iridescent quality. The term 'shot' in this context refers to the weaving technique where the warp (lengthwise) and weft (crosswise) threads are of different colours. It can be made from silk or synthetic fibres.
- **Flocked organza**. The majority of flocking that you will find on fabrics will be synthetic. It is made of tiny fibres stuck to the fabric with a glue in various shapes and patterns. I use a particular type of flocked organza called snow foam or snow dot. The organza is pale blue in colour with a random scatter of white dots of varying sizes. Despite what the name suggests, I find it very useful when representing sea wash or sea spray.

Organza can be difficult to work with because of its lightweight silky properties. Cutting it precisely with scissors, especially for small or thin shapes, can be problematic. If you struggle to cut the shapes you want, you can temporarily attach some stabiliser to the back, but this would need to be removed before stitching the organza in place.

Organza also tends to slip and slide around as it's worked on so you will need to secure your cut shapes in place before stitching. I prefer to use temporary fabric adhesive spray to do this, as it keeps the fabric exactly where I want it. However, when spraying organza, you do have to make sure that you keep the spray nozzle about 20–30cm away and give a short, sharp burst of spray along the piece. Getting too close or being over cautious when depressing the nozzle can result in stringy glue or wet patches,

either of which will be likely to remain visible in your finished work.

For coastal artworks, my main use for organza is when blending the colours in the sea. Organza has a shimmer that effectively represents the sparkle of the water, particularly when you are trying to portray a lovely sunny day in your piece. By using organza on top of other fabric strips such as cotton that I have already layered, it helps to further soften the colours and give the piece a painterly, blended look. I do sometimes use it in the sky as well, depending on the mood I want to create, but if I do that it is usually just as an occasional piece in amongst various layers of fine, non-shiny, coloured net.

Fine coloured net

Unlike organza, net fabric tends to have a much more matt finish. Usually made from synthetic fibres, they come in an array of colours and weights, but I prefer to use fine, lightweight nets in my work for their subtlety. In my seascapes I use such net principally to shade the sky, cutting pieces in various colours and layering them over the base fabric I have used until I am happy with the effect. Depending on the shapes you have cut and where you want to place them, you can either stitch through each piece using invisible thread or, alternatively, cut pieces that can all be stitched at the top – where the stitching will be out of sight once the piece is mounted and framed. As each piece you cut will be a different length you can then allow them to just hang down so the nets blend seamlessly together.

On occasion, I do use nets in the sea as well, particularly if I am trying to represent a grey, misty day.

NEVER IRON ORGANZA!

Do not iron directly onto any organza or net as it will not only melt, but it will also stick to the base of your iron and will be very difficult to remove. Instead, place a clean piece of cotton or linen over the top to protect the fabric first.

HOW TO ADD TEXTURE THROUGH FABRIC MANIPULATION

Certain fabrics lend themselves to assorted manipulation techniques, where interesting and unusual results can be achieved. I'm sure most of you will have come across and perhaps even used techniques such as quilting or appliqué, but other techniques, such as embellishing and heat manipulation, can also be used to great effect.

Using an embellishing machine

An embellishing machine, often referred to as a needle-felting machine or embellisher, looks a lot like a sewing machine and is controlled in the same way by using a foot pedal, but that is where the similarity ends. Instead of the single needle of a sewing machine, an embellisher uses a barrel containing several barbed needles (how many needles will depend on the make of the machine, but it can vary from 5 to 12). It works by mechanically entangling fibres in the fabric through repeated needle-punching. It can be used to add texture, embellishments and fibres to fabrics, as well as create a more weathered and distressed feel to certain materials. I will often use it where I want to add fibres such as silk throwsters to a piece of fabric without stitching them in place. I also frequently use the technique on organza for my abstract seascape to add texture to a material that is typically quite flat.

Using the embellishing machine to create texture on a piece of chiffon.

Heat manipulation

A crafter's heat gun is also a useful tool to have on hand. When used on synthetic fabrics it enables you to produce some very interesting textural results. It can cause the materials to melt, pucker and bubble, producing unique distorted pieces that will certainly add interest to your work. I use a 320W mini heat gun that produces a temperature of 350°C, and find that this is ideal for my needs. It has a fold-down stand which means I can use it hands-free if I wish.

However, before you get started with using a heat gun it is important to consider a few precautions, so it can be used safely.

⬧ Always follow the manufacturer's instructions for your specific heat gun.
⬧ Cover your work surface with a heat-resistant material before you start.
⬧ Only use your heat gun in a well-ventilated room or outside to prevent any build-up of fumes.
⬧ Before working on your main fabric, test the heat gun on a scrap piece to understand how the fabric will react to the heat.
⬧ Make sure that the heat gun is a minimum of 2.5cm away from the fabric at all times to prevent overheating.
⬧ Keep your hands well away from the area of material you are working on. When using the heat gun on small pieces of material either wear heat-proof gloves or hold the fabric down with a utensil, such as metal tongs or a metal knitting needle, to avoid burning your fingers.
⬧ Move the heat gun in a smooth, continuous motion over the fabric. Avoid focusing on one spot for too long to prevent scorching or burning.
⬧ After use, unplug and keep your hands away from the nozzle until it has cooled.
⬧ Allow the heat-manipulated fabric to cool completely before handling or sewing.

Pieces of organza being manipulated with a heat gun.

It is worth noting that natural fabrics such as cotton and linen do not react in the same way as synthetics to heat, and if you use a heat gun on these fabrics they will probably just scorch or burn.

The effects I get and the fabrics I have used will influence where I incorporate them into my work. The majority of my heat-manipulated fabrics are used in my abstract seascapes where my objective is all about representing the coast with colour and texture. Here, heat-manipulated organza works particularly well as it gives a sense of movement which replicates the movement of the water.

In representational pieces there are generally fewer opportunities for using heat manipulation; however, fabric that has been bubbled can depict rocks and pebbles effectively, especially when the colours are appropriate.

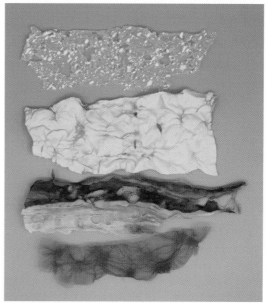

A selection of fabrics showing the interesting effects achieved by heat manipulation.

CHAPTER 5

CREATING A SIMPLE SMALL SEASCAPE

I f you're new to the world of textile art and haven't tried your hand at creating pictures with fabric and stitch before, a small and simple design is the perfect starting point. This approach allows you to gradually become familiar with the necessary techniques, providing a gentle introduction to the art. As you gain experience, you'll find yourself growing in confidence, and eventually you'll be ready to tackle larger, more intricate projects.

In this project, I'll take you step-by-step through the process of constructing a simple seascape design, beginning at the top with the sky and working downward. We'll start by incorporating a simple headland in the distance, and from there we'll gradually build up the scene, first creating the sea and then the beach, before turning our attention to the foreground and some coastal foliage. The end result will be a pretty little coastal scene to frame and be proud of.

This is, of course, just a single example, and I'm sure that once you've completed this project, you'll be eager to explore further and experiment with unique designs of your own. The key for a project of this size is to maintain simplicity; it's easy for a small piece to become busy and overworked, so remember, less is definitely more. Get creative and enjoy experimenting and creating your own designs too!

Step-by-step instructions for producing a 12cm × 12cm seascape

What you will need

- A sewing machine and items from your basic sewing kit (*see* Chapter 2).
- A selection of cotton or other lightweight fabrics in blue, beige and green for the sky, sea and sand. It's a good idea to have some plain fabrics and some with a small floral pattern or design on them.
- A piece of backing fabric 30cm × 30cm.
- A small selection of tiny fabric scraps for the coastal foliage. I would suggest some cotton ditsy florals, loose-weave lightweight tweeds and muslin or scrim in beige, green or pink.
- Two or three different shades of blue organza, ranging from dark to light.
- A piece of mulberry bark or some white lace.
- A spool of white bobbin fill for your bobbin.
- A spool of invisible thread suitable for use in a sewing machine. Alternatively, you could use a selection of coloured threads compatible with your chosen fabrics.
- A matt (mount) with an aperture of 12in × 12in.
- A frame, glazed with glass or Perspex® that will fit the matt. Most off-the-peg frames come with a matt included.
- A piece of pressure-adhesive mount board, cut to the same size as the matt.

OPPOSITE: A work in progress on my sewing table.

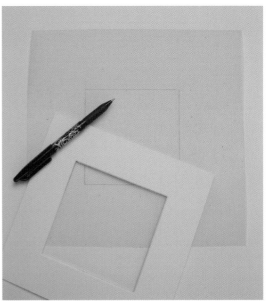

Step 1: Collect together a selection of suitably coloured fabrics. I would suggest a combination of plain and patterned cottons, or other lightweight fabrics.

Step 2: Draw the outline of your working area onto your backing fabric using a heat-erasable pen. You can either use your matt (mount) as a template or make a template out of paper or card to the size you require.

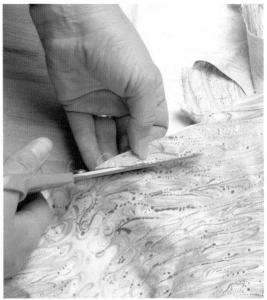

Step 3: I usually begin a piece with the sky. Cut a suitably coloured piece of fabric about 15cm wide and 7cm deep. When offered up over the outline on your backing fabric, the piece of fabric should overlap the edges by about 1cm on three sides.

Step 4: Next we are going to add a headland. You will require a piece of suitably coloured fabric, about 1.5cm deep and 8–9cm wide, tapering off to a point. This can be patterned or plain depending on what fabric you have to hand.

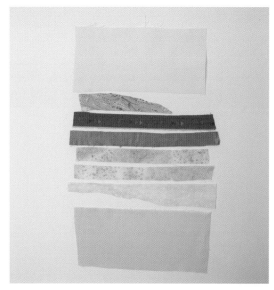

Step 5: Now cut four or five strips to represent the sea. These should each be about 15cm wide by 1.5cm deep and vary in shade from dark to light. The last, lighter piece needs to taper from 3cm deep at one end to 1.5cm at the other. Again, these can be patterned or plain, but if you do use patterned fabric make sure that any pattern is small.

Step 6: Finally cut your area of sand. Again, this needs to be 15cm wide and about 6cm deep. You should now have a set of pieces that look like this.

Step 7: Leaving aside the sand for the moment, place the pieces upside down on a piece of old plastic or cardboard and lightly spray them with a temporary fabric adhesive.

Step 8: Starting with the sky and working downwards, place each piece onto the backing fabric, overlapping them slightly as you go.

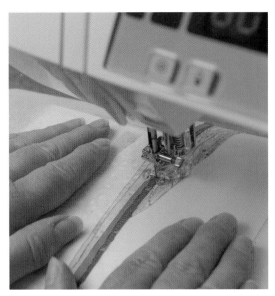

Step 9: Now set up your sewing machine for free-motion embroidery with clear thread on top and white 'bobbin fill' in the bobbin. Start stitching at the top of the sky above your marked line, where the stitches will be out of sight. Then stitch along the top of each piece of fabric in turn. Do not stitch the bottom of the last piece of fabric.

Step 10: Next take the piece of fabric you will use to represent the sand and spray the back with temporary fabric adhesive. Lifting up the bottom edge of the fabric representing the sea, lay the sand in place, smoothing it out as you go.

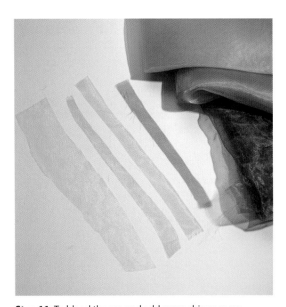

Step 11: To blend the sea and add some shimmer, we now cut three or four pieces of organza. They will need to measure approximately 15cm × 2cm, with one measuring approximately 15cm × 2cm tapering to 4cm.

Step 12: Spray the organza strips with temporary fabric adhesive and lay them, overlapping each other slightly, onto the sea strips already in place. The large, shaped piece of organza should overlap the edge of the sea where it joins the sand. Now stitch the strips of organza in place. As before, do not stitch the bottom of the last piece of organza.

Step 13: To add waves I use a material called bleached mulberry bark. You can pull this apart to get wave-like shapes that you then place onto the sea. Remember waves in the distance will be smaller than waves in the foreground. Secure the waves in place with free-motion stitching, using a zigzag stitch with a width of 1mm.

Step 14: Returning to the sky, add some simple shading with a couple of pieces of coloured net. Layer them however you feel looks best and then stitch along the top (above your marked line) to secure them in place.

Step 15: Gather together a selection of small fabric scraps in foliage colours, that include lightweight cotton fabrics and some loose-weave pieces. Ideally, these should be a combination of plain colours and small floral or patterned pieces.

Step 16: Cut some small randomly shaped pieces. Remember that what you want to end up with is a *representation* of vegetation, not a botanically accurate recreation, so don't be too precise.

Step 17: Manipulate the loose-weave fabric pieces to make them look more natural. Remove the weft from part of the fabric and then cut into the warp to give the impression of grasses.

Step 18: Place your pieces of fabric along the bottom of your seascape so that the lower edges will be hidden behind the matt (mount) when finished. Keep offering up the matt until you are happy with the composition.

Step 19: Take a photograph of the layout before removing the pieces to spray, as this will help you to put them back in the correct order. Spray the backs of the pieces with temporary fabric adhesive and place them back onto your picture using the photo you took as a guide. I don't tend to spray loose-weave pieces as they will stay in place on their own until stitched because of their fibrous nature.

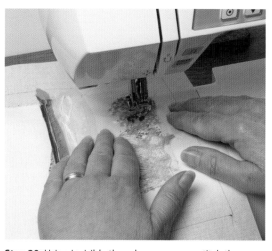

Step 20: Using invisible thread, you can now stitch these pieces in place. Try not to stitch across them in a straight line, instead use a wiggly line that will blend into the fabrics and add to the texture. Your piece is now ready for framing (*see* Chapter 9).

Your picture is now finished and ready for framing (*see* Chapter 9).

Now that you've created one picture, why not try some more? Below are a few ideas on how you can change the foreground when creating further pieces. Just remember that whatever you add to the foreground must be in proportion to the rest of the piece. Of course, you may also decide to keep the overall composition the same and just change the colours of the fabrics.

Here you can see the finished piece in a white wood frame. I have used a thick matt (mount) to set back the artwork and keep it from touching the glass.

This photograph shows a similar seascape but with a 'strandline' running across the beach area. This is made up of thread offcuts, seed beads and French knots. Working on such a small piece you only need a few threads and beads as you want to keep the correct scale of the strandline relative to the beach. I have couched down the threads by hand, using invisible thread instead of using the sewing machine as this gives a more natural look.

In this variation I have added rocks and pebbles in the foreground using a combination of fabric, buttons and beads. I machine-stitched the pieces of fabric in place first and then hand-stitched on the beads and buttons. When working with beads and buttons like this, it is a good idea to place everything out first so that you are happy with the composition, and then take a photograph on your phone that you can refer to whilst stitching everything in place.

Here you can see that I have used a foliage foreground, similar to the step-by-step project piece. However, this time I have added a fence (see Chapter 8 for instructions). Because of the small size of the piece I have used floristry wire for the fence posts, poking them down behind the foliage which was stitched in place first using the machine. Then I used two strands of silver hand embroidery thread for the cross wires which hold the posts in place.

CHAPTER 6

WORKING ON A LARGER SCALE

Creating something on a larger scale can be very rewarding, but it does come with new challenges. Although some of the processes are pretty much the same as with smaller pieces, a larger scale does allow you to experiment with more elaborate compositions, enabling you to incorporate details that may not be feasible in smaller formats. However, really large pieces can sometimes be difficult to handle, especially when it comes to getting them under the sewing machine for stitching. Therefore, I would recommend a gradual increase in size rather than jumping from smaller to significantly larger pieces. This approach will provide you with the opportunity to refine your skills and techniques over time.

While working on a larger scale does require a greater investment of time and effort, the increased size will bring an increased sense of achievement once it is completed.

I very rarely draw out my composition before starting a new piece of textile art, but I would suggest that for larger pieces you consider doing so, as with all that extra space to fill it can be very easy to lose sight of where things need to go, and you could easily end up with a composition that doesn't work.

The following project is 228mm × 432mm (9in × 17in) in size and gives you a portrait format seascape with cliffs and sea in the distance and a curving beach that runs into the foreground. This is a great composition for showing depth and perspective and will incorporate many processes that will help you develop your skills further.

The piece is inspired by a photograph I took along the Jurassic coast.

A view of the Jurassic coast between Lyme Regis and Charmouth in Dorset. (Photo: Alison Whateley)

OPPOSITE: My piece entitled *Sea Fret* depicts a misty morning on the beach. (Photo: Alison Whateley)

Step-by-step guide to producing a larger piece

What you will need

- A sewing machine and items from your basic sewing kit (*see* Chapter 2).
- A selection of fabrics in coastal colours. I would recommend a variety of weights including some sheer fabrics for shading. Also some neutral-coloured lightweight lace and a tiny amount of bleached mulberry bark.
- A small amount of polyester wadding (optional).
- Embellishment materials to include a selection of buttons, beads and hand embroidery threads.
- A piece of backing fabric 45cm × 65cm.
- A spool of white bobbin fill for your bobbin.
- A spool of invisible thread suitable for use on a sewing machine. Alternatively, you could use a selection of coloured threads compatible with your chosen fabrics.
- A matt (mount) with an aperture of 228mm × 432mm (9in × 17in).
- A piece of pressure-adhesive mount board, cut to the same size as the matt.

Step 1: Firstly, gather together a selection of fabrics in coastal colours. Here is my initial selection based on the photograph that inspired this project.

Step 2: Place your backing fabric on a flat surface and position your matt centrally, before using a heat erasable pen to draw around the inside. This will give you your working area.

Step 3: Select a suitable piece of fabric for the sky and, using temporary fabric adhesive, spray the back and put it in place. Make sure your fabric piece overlaps the marked area by about a centimetre. Now using a heat erasable pen, draw in the cliffs and sea areas.

Step 4: Using lightweight stabiliser or a piece of double-sided fusible web adhesive, trace the outline of each cliff allowing extra area at the bottom of each piece so that fabrics can be overlapped before stitching.

Step 5: Using the templates you have produced, attach them to the back of your chosen pieces of fabric and cut around them.

Step 6: Slowly build up the cliff area using temporary fabric adhesive to hold each piece in place until stitched. Start at the back and work forward, overlapping each piece slightly.

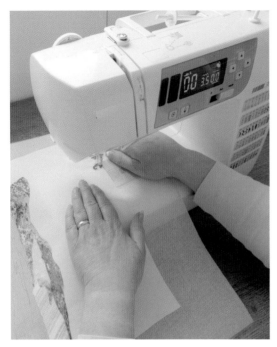

Step 7: Now stitch the top of the sky in place just above the marked line where the mount will sit. This way you will not see this stitching once the piece is mounted and framed.

Step 8: Next stitch the cliff area, but make sure you only stitch the top of the lower pieces of fabric as you will need to lift the base later when adding the beach and sea.

Step 9: Once the cliff area has been stitched, cut your strips of fabric for the sea and secure them in place using temporary fabric adhesive. You will need to lift the base of the cliffs and place your first strip of sea slightly underneath.

Step 10: Now add the start of the sand area. Again, start by lifting the base of the cliffs and tucking the fabric under. Progress down so that the sea is surrounded by tapered strips of sand, making sure to tuck the sand under the sea when you get to that point. Also, add the rocks that jut out into the sea. These need to sit on top of the sand area.

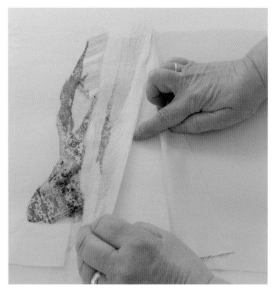

Step 11: Sew these strips of sand, sea and rock in place. Use a few random lines of stitches across the beach, rocks and sea following the contours.

Step 12: The rest of the beach area should now be put in place. Use one piece of suitably coloured fabric cut slightly larger than the marked area. Spray with temporary fabric adhesive and smooth it into place, tucking it under the strips of sand you already have there. You do not need to stitch this at this stage.

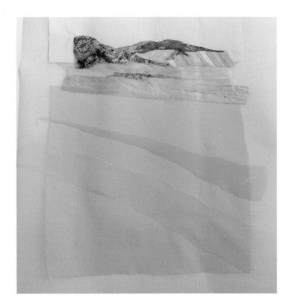

Step 13: Cut a couple of pieces of fine coloured net as seen here. These will be placed at the edge of the sea to represent the darker sand where the waves break. Once positioned correctly, fix them in place with a couple of lines of stitching.

Step 14: To represent the distant pebbled area on the beach, use some fine slightly patterned lace cut into randomly shaped pieces that can be positioned to represent the curve of the bay. Stitch the pieces in place once you are happy with their distribution.

Step 15: Use a selection of different patterned and plain fabrics in a variety of weights to represent the pebbles and rocks in the foreground. Cut various rock-like shapes in different sizes and place them on your piece of work until you are happy with the composition. Offer up your matt (mount) regularly to ensure the rocks will be correctly placed in your finished composition. Remember to place the larger rocks at the front to give a sense of depth.

Step 16: Once you are happy with the placement, you need to stitch your rock and pebbles in place. For those in the foreground, you may want to use some wadding to increase the sense of shape. Here I am using a knitting needle to push wadding under the rock as I stitch around it.

Step 17: Now you can begin to add the embellishments. I have used various buttons and beads. Experiment with the placement of these and when happy I would suggest taking a photo to remind yourself of where each one goes. Stitch these in place with invisible thread.

Step 18: Next, you can add the seed beads and French knots. Again, experiment with the placement, but placing the smaller embellishments on the distant beach will enhance a sense of depth. I would suggest using a heat erasable pen to mark the position of each bead and knot, as with items this small you will find it difficult to see them in a photograph.

Step 19: The waves can be represented by using bleached mulberry bark. You will need very little as the waves will appear small on the distant sea. Stitch these pieces in place with either free-motion zigzag stitch or hand stitch using invisible thread.

Step 20: To add interest to the sky, you can now add some pieces of fine coloured net or pale organza to create shading. These pieces should vary in shape and be secured by a line of stitching at the top edge of the piece.

Here you can see the finished, mounted piece, ready for framing.

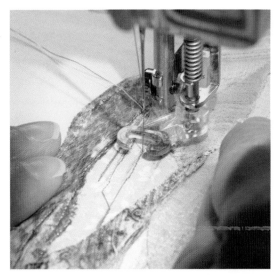

Step 21: I have added some areas of coloured stitched detail to the cliffs and fields, but this is entirely optional and will depend on what fabrics you have used.

The finished piece has been mounted on board and is shown here with a matt in place, ready for framing. You can see how the eye travels from the foreground, along the curve of the beach towards the distant headland.

CHAPTER 7

CREATING A SEMI-ABSTRACT SEASCAPE

Semi-abstract art emerged in the early twentieth century as artists sought new ways to express themselves beyond traditional realism and strict abstraction. Like abstract art, it is a departure from traditional representation but still maintains some connection to reality by incorporating recognisable elements.

I find it quite a liberating way to work as it's an opportunity to explore texture, colour and movement without the constraints of representing a view. Colours have the remarkable ability to convey mood, evoke emotions and enhance the viewer's connection to the artwork, so whether you choose to experiment with bold and vibrant shades of blues and greens to capture the energy of the sea, or go for a more subdued palette to convey a sense of calm and tranquillity, the choice is yours. Remember too that seascapes are not just about the sea, so consider incorporating the varied colours of the beach into your artwork as well – this can contribute to the overall mood and authenticity of your coastal composition.

If you've got a box of fabric scraps then this sort of project is definitely one you should try, as it's great for using up those small pieces that many people would throw away (you knew you were keeping them all for a reason didn't you?). It also means that you are likely to have access to a wider variety of fabrics in various weights, textures and colours which will help to give your finished piece more interest.

As well as using textured fabrics, you can also create both texture and movement from the way you lay the materials down. Lightweight fabrics are particularly easy to manipulate if you want to create the undulations of the sea or the textures of the sand. I will often spray these pieces with temporary fabric adhesive and then pinch and bend them as I lay them in place, stitching them down with invisible thread to create the desired effect. This is just one way of manipulating them, but you may want to try altering the texture of some fabrics by using an embellishing machine or heat gun to achieve different effects (*see* Chapter 8).

When it comes to adding embellishments, it is easy to get carried away. Beach-combing finds are an obvious choice but use your imagination to gather a selection of things that will add to the coastal feel of the piece. Know when to stop though, as you don't want to overload your work. As discussed in the next chapter, I only incorporate embellishments that I can stitch in place, but if you would prefer to glue them in position then that is fine.

In this chapter, I will be focusing on creating a semi-abstract piece based on the coastline where the sea meets the shore. Embrace the freedom to express your creativity whilst still incorporating recognisable elements that belong to a coastal setting.

I encourage you to view this project as a starting point for experimenting with unique

OPPOSITE: My abstract seascape *Littoral* depicts the rich colours and textures of the sea and beach. (Photo: Southgate Studios)

ideas and techniques of your own. While you can choose to closely follow the step-by-step instructions, there's no obligation to do so. Feel free to use the steps and techniques as a foundation for creating your individual interpretation of the coast.

Step-by-step instructions for creating a semi-abstract seascape

What you will need

- A sewing machine and items from your basic sewing kit (*see* Chapter 2).
- A spool of white bobbin fill and a reel of invisible thread suitable for use in a sewing machine.
- A piece of backing fabric and a piece of lightweight quilter's batting, both measuring approximately 18cm × 18cm. The finished piece will measure approximately 20cm × 20cm.

- A selection of suitable plain and patterned materials. Medium and lightweight fabrics work best as they are easier to manipulate. However, think outside the box when selecting, you don't have to stick to fabric, you can use any suitable material as long as it can be stitched in place.
- A selection of embellishments. I have used sea glass, buttons, seed beads, silk cocoons, shells, driftwood, tree bark, a metal washer, tiny metal rings and fisherman's twine. You don't have to go out and source all these things, just experiment with what you have to hand.
- A few coloured threads (variegated ones work well) if you want to add any stitched detail to your work. Although I initially selected some, I didn't end up using them for this piece.
- A piece of plain (non-adhesive) mount board no less than 36cm × 36cm.

Step 1: Collect together an initial selection of materials, embellishments and threads suitable for representing the coast. Note that my selection includes both plain and patterned fabrics. You may not use them all, and you may want to add to the initial selection as you progress with the piece, but this will give you a good starting point.

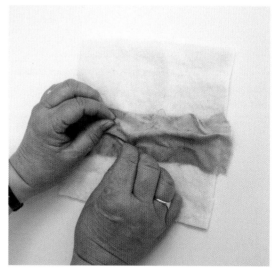

Step 2: Place your piece of quilter's batting on top of your piece of backing fabric. Then selecting one piece of material at a time, spray the back with temporary fabric adhesive and lay it onto the batting in the position you would like it to be (any pieces that start or finish at the edge need to overhang it by about 1cm). I have started in the middle of my piece, and am pinching the fabric to create extra texture, but you can start wherever you like.

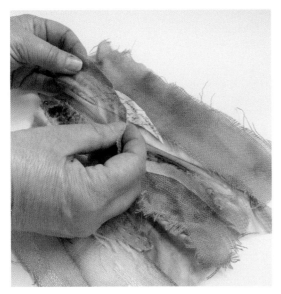

Step 3: Continue to build up the background by adding further pieces. Make sure that the pieces are overlapping slightly so that you don't have any gaps once it is finished. Here you can see that the majority of the batting is now covered.

Step 4: Now you can see that the batting is completely covered. To represent the coastal theme, I have used a selection of fabric pieces in shades of cream, beige and pale blue. Note the different weights and textures of the fabric pieces.

Step 5: With your sewing machine set up for free-motion sewing and threaded with invisible thread, stitch each piece of fabric in place. Usually one line of stitching through the middle of each piece is enough, but if you have wider pieces they may need to be stitched a bit more. The important thing is not to add too much stitching at this stage, as it is purely about holding the fabrics in place.

Step 6: Now you can turn your attention to adding sheer fabrics such as organza and net to blend the initial background and further develop the piece. If you want the organza to have more texture, you can heat manipulate it using a craft heat gun (*see* Chapter 8 for how to do this).

Step 7: Now I am returning the work to the sewing machine and with invisible thread as before, I am stitching the organza in place. If you chose to use temporary fabric adhesive on your sheer fabrics, make sure to give them a very light spray from about 20cm away so as not to get wet, gluey stains on the fabric, which may show once the piece is finished.

Step 8: Your piece should now look something like this. The background is completed and you are now ready to move on to the next stage, which is adding the embellishments.

Step 9: I have decided to use a few small pieces of tree bark to represent rocks. I have pierced a couple of holes in each piece so that I can then stitch them in place. To do this, thread up a needle with invisible thread and stitch them in place by hand.

Step 10: Here you can see that I have developed the piece further by adding more embellishments. This is adding both interest and texture. You can add whatever you have available that you feel will work, but I have added silk carrier rods, shells, sea glass, fisherman's twin and silk cocoons. Place them where you feel they work best for your piece.

Step 11: Once all the larger embellishments have been stitched in place, I complete the finishing touches by adding a few smaller pieces. Here I am using a size 10 beading needle to add a scattering of seed beads.

Step 12: My finished semi-abstract representation of where the sea meets the shore is full of texture and interest.

When it comes to displaying rough-edged pieces like this, I would suggest framing them in such a way that the rough edges are still visible, as these are part of the character of the piece. For full instructions on how to do this please refer to Chapter 9.

CHAPTER 8

ADDING HAND STITCHING AND MIXED MEDIA

I often use hand embroidery stitches and mixed media items to add texture and interest to my seascapes. What and how much I add depends on both the size of the piece and the composition as a whole. You will find that, whereas some pieces are enhanced by these additions, others are better without, and knowing what to add where and when is something that becomes easier with experience.

I think we all have a bit of the magpie within us, and the temptation to use a bit of everything can sometimes be hard to resist, especially when it comes to sparkly things! However, generally speaking, a few carefully selected additions will have more impact on your finished piece than overloading it.

ADDING HAND EMBROIDERY STITCHES

Hand embroidery is a timeless and intricate form of needlework that has a rich history spanning thousands of years. It has been used to embellish textiles, create decorative art and convey cultural and personal stories. Although there are many different hand embroidery stitches, there are two that I use frequently in my work: the French knot and the bullion knot. These make very useful additions when added to my seascapes and help to add texture and interest.

I use them to represent small pebbles and shells on the beach. They are ideal for when you want to add small details in the distance that just give an impression of what might be there.

I also use them in my smaller works to represent sea thrifts and other coastal flora, and it's a great way to add a pop of colour to a coastal piece.

OPPOSITE: A detail from my textile artwork *Indigo Waters* showing the effective use of mixed media and other embellishments. (Photo: Alison Whateley)

Step-by-step guide to creating a French knot

Stitching a French knot is a basic embroidery technique used to create small, textured dots or knots on fabric.

For this stitch, you need a medium-length needle with a small eye.

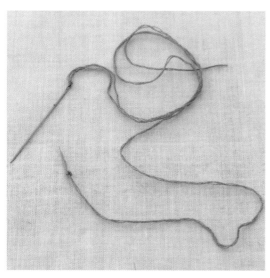

Step 1: Thread your needle with embroidery thread and tie a knot at the end (I usually use two or three strands).

Step 2: Starting with the needle at the back of the fabric, bring it up through the fabric to the top until the thread is stopped by the knot.

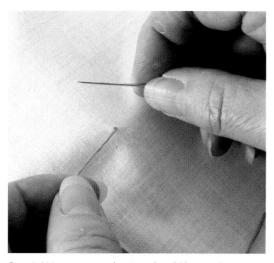

Step 3: Using your non-dominant hand (the one that is not holding the needle), hold the threat taut between your thumb and forefinger around 5cm from where it comes through the fabric.

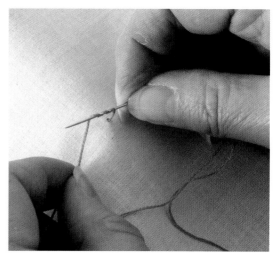

Step 4: Wrap the thread around the needle a few times. (I usually use two or three turns – the more times you wind it around the needle, the larger the knot will be.)

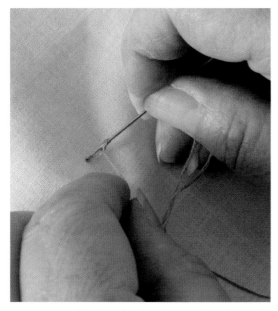

Step 5: Now, still holding the thread taut, replace the needle into the fabric just beside the point it came up.

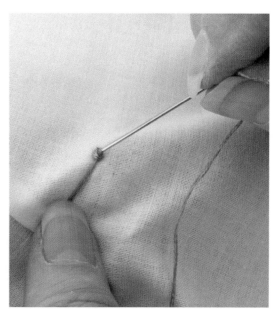

Step 6: Finally, pull the coiled thread to tighten it up and slide it down the needle so it sits on the surface of the fabric.

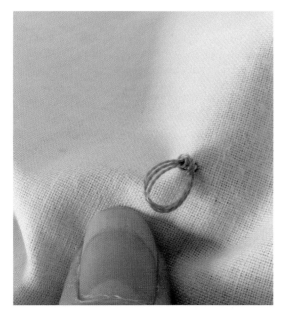

Step 7: Pull the needle all the way through and cast off on the underside of the fabric.

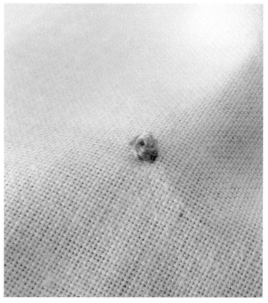

Step 8: The finished French knot sits neatly on the surface of the fabric.

Practice is the key to perfecting your French knot technique. It may take a few tries to get the tension and appearance of the knots just right, but with patience, you'll be able to create beautiful textured areas in your textile art projects.

Step-by-step guide to creating bullion knots

A bullion knot is a decorative embroidery stitch that resembles a small length of coiled or twisted rope.

To create this stitch, you need a long needle with a small eye.

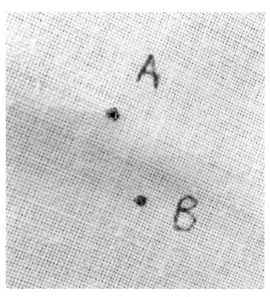

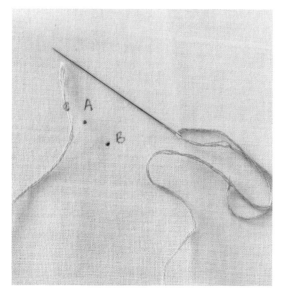

Step 1: Decide where you want your knot to be, and how long you want it. Mark two dots on the fabric to indicate where it will start and finish (I have marked the two points A and B in this illustration).

Step 2: Thread your needle with some embroidery thread and tie a knot at one end (I use two or three strands).

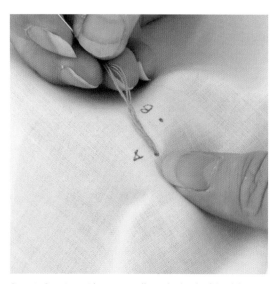

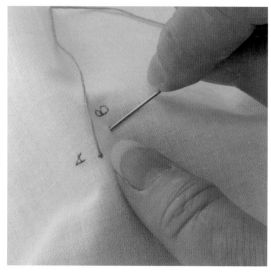

Step 3: Starting with your needle at the back of the fabric, bring it up through the fabric at point A and pull the thread through until it is stopped by the knot.

Step 4: Then put the needle back into the fabric at point B. Push the needle all the way through, but not the thread.

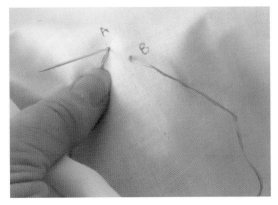

Step 5: Bring the needle back through the fabric just beside point A, but don't pull it all the way through.

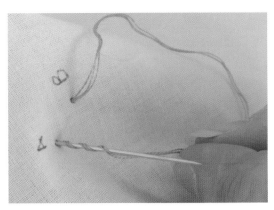

Step 6: Next, using your non-dominant hand, wind the thread around the needle enough times to fill the distance between A and B.

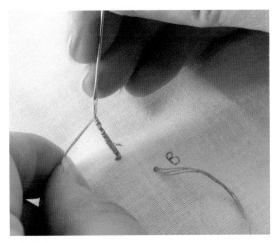

Step 7: Now, holding the coils tightly with your non-dominant hand, carefully start to bring up the needle and thread through the coils and use your non-dominant hand to form the stitch.

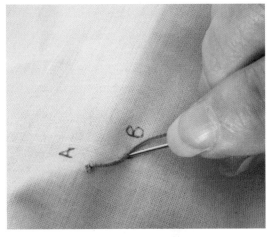

Step 8: Finally, push the needle back through the fabric at point B and cast off on the underside of the fabric.

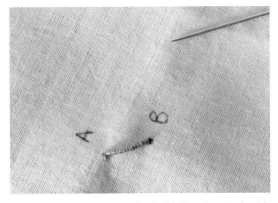

Step 9: Here you can see the finished bullion knot. It should lay flat against the fabric.

Bullion knots can be a bit tricky at first, so practice is essential to master this stitch. Adjust the number of coils and the tightness of them to achieve the desired look for your project. With time and patience, you'll be able to create beautiful bullion knots to enhance your designs.

ADDING BUTTONS, BEADS AND SEQUINS

Using buttons, beads and sequins in your seascapes can add depth, texture and a touch of sparkle to your creations. These embellishments offer a wide range of creative possibilities, allowing you to experiment with colours and shapes. Combine your beads and sequins with some French and bullion knots to represent the mixture of shingle and shells on the shoreline.

USING BEACHCOMBING FINDS

I love to incorporate a few beachcombing finds in my seascapes if the composition allows, as these objects create a direct connection to the coast, and add a sense of authenticity to those pieces. You may want to include shells that you have collected from your local beach – or those which have come from somewhere that holds a special place in your heart. Maybe they evoke memories of a wonderful holiday or

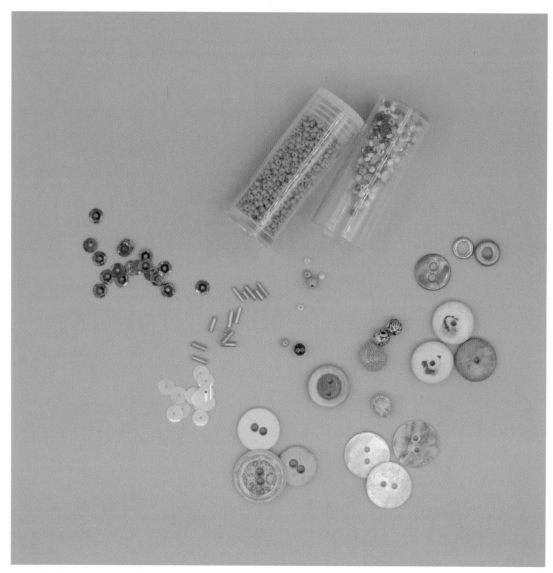

A varied selection of embellishments including buttons, beads and sequins are useful for bringing your work to life.

remind you of time spent with someone special. Incorporating these into a piece of artwork you have created yourself will serve as a reminder of where and when they were collected. This is particularly true if the piece is your representation of that place.

Firstly though, a note of caution regarding what you can take from the beach. We all love a bit of beachcombing, and I will often incorporate finds in my artwork. It is, however, important to be aware that individual countries will have different rules on what you can and can't take from the beach, so please check local regulations.

In the UK, the Coast Protection Act 1949 made it illegal to remove natural materials from any beach (there isn't currently any UK-wide law that protects driftwood and shells, but do check by-laws for any local restrictions). The 1949 act exists to protect our beaches from erosion and to maintain their natural habitat and ecosystems, which is, of course, in everyone's interest. Pebbles and sand are obviously off-limits, but beyond that, as regards natural materials, it is about using a bit of common sense and restraint. Empty shells and small pieces of driftwood are fine if by-laws permit but be sure to check that shells are no longer

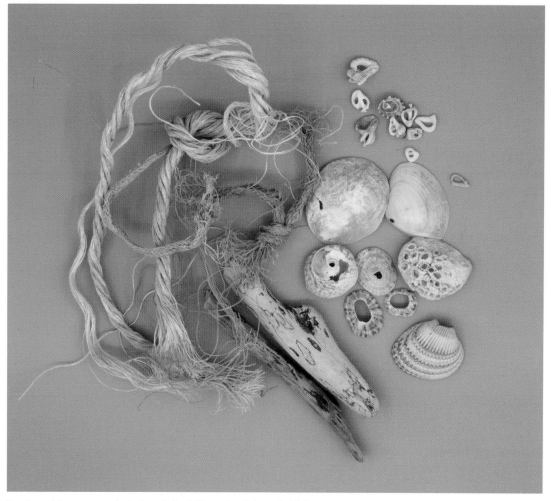

Beachcombing treasures including shells, driftwood and discarded fishing twine help to create a connection to the subject of the picture.

inhabited. Take only what you will use, as both shells and driftwood can provide homes for a variety of small creatures.

When it comes to sea glass, beach plastics and metals, you can take as much as you want as they are not naturally occurring materials and are potentially hazardous to marine wildlife.

Cleaning and disinfecting beach finds

Before using any beach finds in your artwork, cleaning and disinfecting them is essential. It is a responsible and practical step to preserve them and prevent cross-contamination. So, let's look at how to clean and disinfect your beach finds to make it safe to use them in your artwork.

Sea glass

Sea glass is quite straightforward. I would recommend nothing more than a quick rinse in some hot soapy water, before leaving them out to dry thoroughly.

Shells

I personally prefer to clean shells in much the same way as sea glass, although they may also need a light scrub with a small brush to remove any debris such as sand from their nooks and crannies. It's worth noting that I only collect shells that are already in good, clean condition. This means I avoid picking up shells that have an unpleasant odour or are covered in slimy seaweed and other debris. Shells in such a state would require more thorough disinfection, which can be more complex and a time-consuming process.

Driftwood

Even if your small pieces of driftwood look spotless, it is still important to clean and disinfect them before using them in your art. Start by giving your pieces a light sand or brush to remove any loose debris. Then, as I prefer not to use bleach, I soak them in a solution of

250ml of white vinegar to 4.5 litres of water for a day or so. Vinegar has natural cleaning properties and can help remove dirt and kill bacteria. Rinse thoroughly and allow them to dry completely before incorporating them into your work.

USING RUSTY METAL

When it comes to incorporating rusty metal in a seascape artwork, I would not suggest using large pieces that are severely rusted and crumbling. However, it is possible to incorporate small pieces such as rusty washers and nails that you may find in the garden shed, or items like bottle tops, can-tops and ring-pulls that may have washed up on the beach. As with all the other found objects I add to my artwork, these will first need a good clean. Using a wire brush or piece of sandpaper I begin by removing any loose rust and dirt. Be careful not to over-clean, though, as you will want to retain the weathered character.

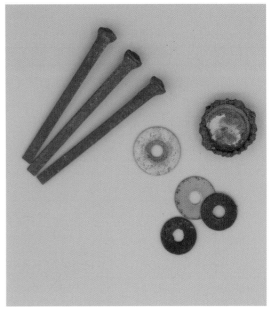

Pieces of rusty metal suitable for incorporating into your artwork evoke the way the sea weathers and corrodes material discarded by man.

After cleaning, I wash the pieces in warm water with a mild detergent before leaving them on an old piece of cloth to dry thoroughly.

If you want to stabilise your pieces to prevent further corrosion, you can apply a rust converter according to the manufacturer's instructions. This step can help seal the rust and create a protective layer. However, I don't usually feel the need to use this as it can change the colour. Instead, to protect the fabric on my artwork from being degraded by the rusty metal over time I apply a coat or two of clear matt varnish. Once you're satisfied with the preparation you can incorporate the rusty metal into your textile art.

Remember that rusted metal can add a unique and weathered aesthetic to your textile art. Embrace the imperfections and textures that rust brings, as they can contribute to the character and visual interest of your artwork.

HOW I INCORPORATE MIXED MEDIA ITEMS

My personal preference when adding mixed media to my work is to stitch it in place. Therefore, I only select items where this is possible. I collect shells from the beach that are either broken or have holes in them and collect driftwood that is either soft enough to pierce a couple of holes through or has a slight split that will allow for my thread to slide in and hold it tightly. With sea glass, you will need to drill a small hole in the middle so you can loop the thread through – as you would do with a metal washer. When stitching in mixed media I prefer to use invisible thread as, although it can be fiddly work, I prefer the overall aesthetic.

Using stitching will not be for everyone, and an alternative is to glue your pieces in place using a strong adhesive suitable for use with fabrics. Be careful not to use too much glue, as when you press your piece onto your artwork you want to avoid excess glue spilling out around and becoming visible. You will also need to use museum-quality glue, as many commercially available adhesives can yellow or, more importantly, become brittle with age. Whatever method you use, the most important thing is that your pieces are completely secure and will not become loose over time.

REPRESENTING A FENCE USING MIXED MEDIA AND STITCHING

When it comes to creating a realistic representation of a fence using metal nails and stitching, I have developed a method that ensures that the posts are securely held in place. Here are a few points to consider before you start:

You may want to draw in the placement of the cross wires with a heat-erasable pen so that you have lines to follow.

If you think you might find it hard to hold the fence posts in place at the same time as securing them with the cross thread, you could use invisible thread to secure them first.

You should choose a thread for the cross-wires that is the correct thickness in relation to the size of the posts. For example, I would use a single strand of hand embroidery thread for a small fence. For larger fences, I may use six strands of embroidery thread or perhaps even a thicker cord, such as waxed jewellery cord.

Step-by-step guide to stitching a fence

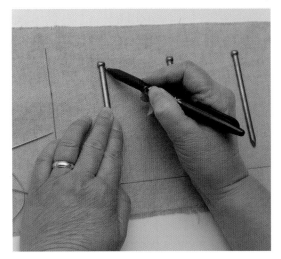

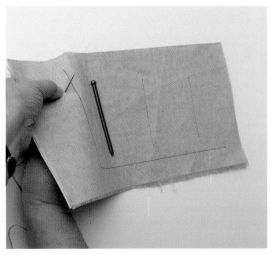

Step 1: Work out where you want your fence posts to go and mark the location with a heat-erasable pen. For seascapes, this is usually in the foreground, as it will represent fencing on the dunes. Make sure that the nails are in proportion to the size of your picture. For really small seascapes, I use cut pieces of floristry wire to represent the posts.

Step 2: Thread up a suitably sized needle with your chosen thread then tie a double knot in the end. Starting from the back of the fabric, bring your needle up where you would like the cross wire to begin. I usually start from the side where the fence will end up outside the edge of the picture, so the starting point will eventually be hidden by the matt.

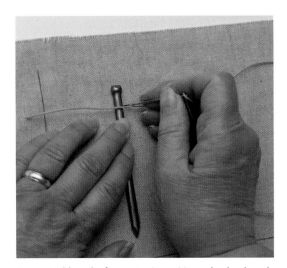

Step 3: Holding the fence post in position, take the thread over it and insert the needle back into the fabric close to the side of the post. Pull the thread right through until it is tight.

Step 4: To stop the post from moving, go underneath to the other side of the post. Then bring the needle up through the fabric tight to the post just above the cross thread. Pull the thread all the way through.

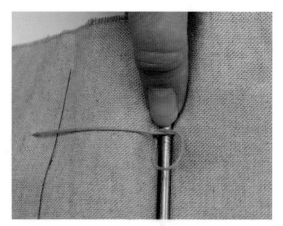

Step 5: Next, re-insert the needle just below the cross thread and pull the thread all the way through until it is tight.

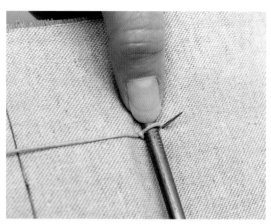

Step 6: Now, to extend the crosswire to the next post, bring the needle up on the other side of the first fence post, in the same place as you took the thread down before.

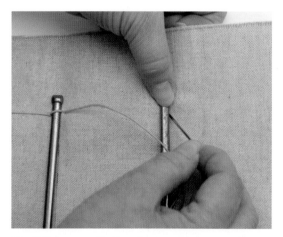

Step 7: You can see the thread going over the second fence post and the needle being inserted into the fabric immediately beside it.

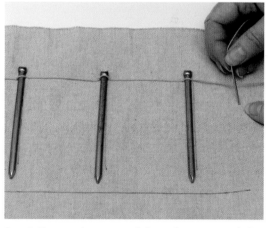

Step 8: Once you have secured all your fence posts with the top crosswire, insert the needle into the fabric as shown, and cast off on the back.

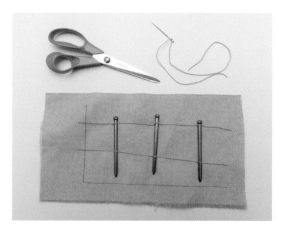

Step 9: Repeat this process for each cross wire. I would recommend using two or three crosswires depending on the size of the fence and the size of your piece.

CHAPTER 9

MOUNTING AND FRAMING

Creating a piece of textile art is not a quick process regardless of its size and, given the time and effort you will have put into your work, it's essential to ensure that your finished piece is displayed in the best possible way. Careful consideration needs to be given when choosing how to display it. There are, of course, many ways that this can be done; what works best will depend on the style of the piece you have created.

Here I will cover the two ways I mount my work, depending on its style.

◆ Standard mounting of textile art refers to a conventional and widely used method of presenting textile artwork in a clean, professional and secure manner. For me, this technique involves securing the textile piece to artist's self-adhesive mount board, before adding a matt (mount) and frame. With this traditional style of mounting all your rough edges are covered up.

◆ Rough-edge mounting of textile art is a creative and unconventional approach to presenting textile artwork. In this technique, the fabric edges are intentionally left in a raw, frayed or unfinished state, and the artwork is mounted in a way that preserves these rough, textured edges. This method is used to achieve a more organic and tactile look, often imparting a sense of rustic charm and visual interest to the piece.

For both styles of mounting my preferred choice is to frame it behind glass. There has long been a debate around whether you should display your textile art behind glass or not, but it is something that I have decided to do as I feel it gives my finished work more protection. Glass serves as a barrier against dust, moisture and physical contact, guarding the art against potential damage over time. Furthermore, framing textile art behind glass often conveys a clear message to viewers that they are looking at a piece of art.

When choosing to frame your artwork behind glass, make certain that your piece does not come into contact with the glass itself, as such contact can lead to damage to your work over time.

Framing behind glass, when done correctly, can not only safeguard your artwork but also enhance it, all the while ensuring the preservation of your hard work for years to come.

MOUNTING YOUR ARTWORK

I will show you two ways to mount your artwork, as discussed above. Which method you will use depends on the type of work you have produced.

OPPOSITE: My textile artwork *Otter Head* was photographed 'on location' at Budleigh Salterton.

Step-by-step guide to preparing and mounting your artwork

If you are going to mount and frame your artwork yourself, you will need the following equipment:

- Iron and ironing pad.
- Craft knife or rotary cutter (I keep an old rotary cutter for doing this – don't use your fabric rotary cutter or you will soon blunt the blade).
- Cutting board.
- Ruler.
- Heat-erasable pen.
- pH-neutral adhesive mount board (pressure activated).

Preparing and mounting your work
The initial step involves preparing your completed artwork for attachment to the adhesive mount board. Proper preparation is essential, as it plays a crucial role in ensuring your artwork appears at its best when displayed on the wall. To achieve this, carefully inspect both the front and back of your piece, eliminating any loose ends or long threads. Pay special attention to the back, as it's crucial to avoid any clumped threads, as they could become visible and spoil the smooth finish you're aiming for once the artwork is affixed to the adhesive mount board.

After completing the aforementioned steps, if you've used a backing fabric treated with a stiffening agent like starch to prevent puckering during stitching, you might want to consider soaking it in warm water to remove this treatment. While not always necessary, this will result in a softer fabric and better adhesion to the adhesive mount board, reducing the

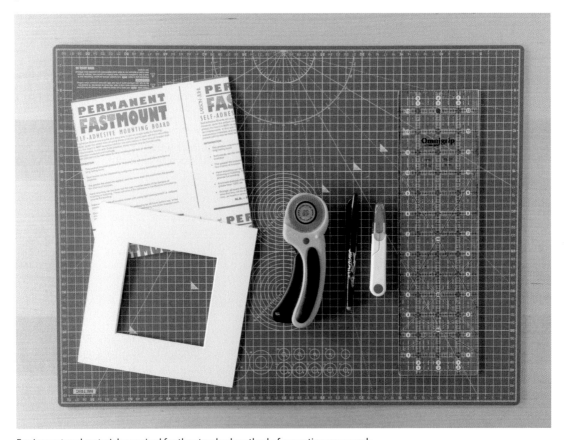

Equipment and materials required for the standard method of mounting your work.

likelihood of it peeling over time. Although it might sound a bit daunting, as long as the materials you've used are colour-fast, there's no need to worry.

After soaking, simply lay the fabric flat on an old towel to let it dry.

When your piece is dry you need to give it a good press. Using a steam iron, I prefer to press my work on the back, laying it face down onto a folded towel or similar material. If the piece has mixed media such as beads or shells that stand proud this is the safest way to press it because it reduces the risk of breakages.

Alternatively, if your piece is fairly smooth you can place a clean piece of cotton or linen over the top before pressing it on the front. Do not use your iron directly onto the front of the artwork as you might risk damaging the piece. This is particularly important if you have used sheer fabrics in your work as the iron will melt them, ruining your work and potentially causing permanent damage to the sole of your iron.

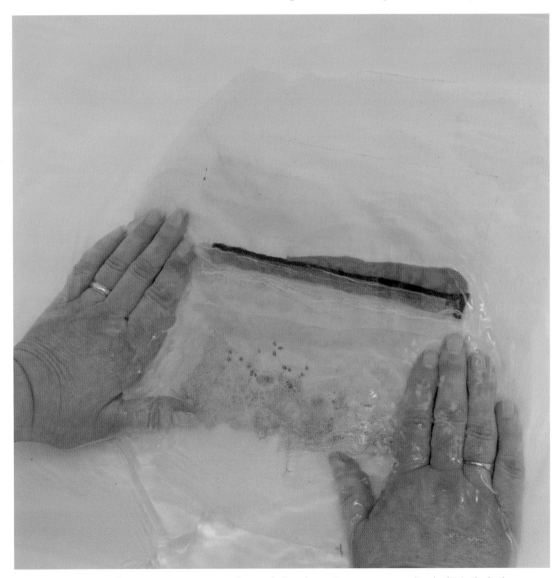

Gently soak your artwork in warm water to remove the starch. For a large piece, you may need to do this in the bath.

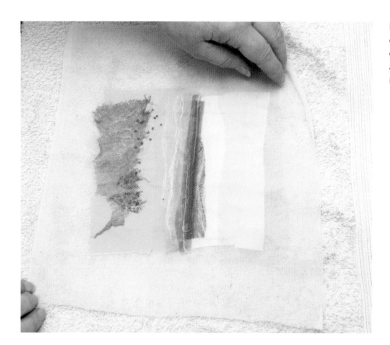

Drain off most of the water and lay out your piece on a towel to dry. Try to gently smooth out most of the creases as it will reduce the amount of ironing needed later.

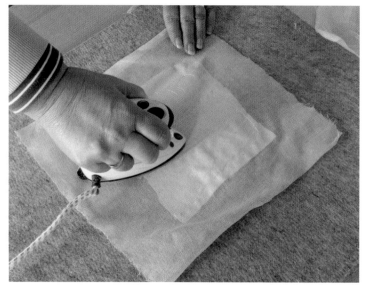

Once your work is dry, press it gently. You can either press on the back of the piece or the front, as described in the text.

If you are using calico or any other backing fabric which has not been sized, you should skip the soaking stage.

Now we come to the actual mounting of your work. Firstly, to make this step as easy as possible, the adhesive mount board needs to be the same size as your matt. Mountboard can usually be purchased in various sizes, so you may be fortunate enough to buy the correct size that won't need any adjustment. If the precise size is not available, purchase the next size up from what you need. Place your matt on top of it and draw around the outside with a pencil or heat-erasable pen. Then remove the matt and, using a ruler and a rotary cutter or craft knife, cut off the excess so you end up with both the matt and the adhesive mount board the same size.

Now you are ready to mount your artwork.

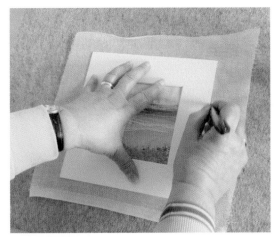

Step 1: Place the matt over your piece so that you are happy with the way the composition is framed. Then, using a heat-erasable pen, draw around the outer edge of the matt. Place the matt to one side.

Step 2: Now take the adhesive mount board and carefully peel back the waxed paper by about 3–4cm at the top to expose the adhesive surface.

Step 3: Taking your finished piece, place the two top corners you marked onto the top two corners of the mount board. Press it down firmly with your hands and smooth out any wrinkles.

Step 4: Continue to gradually pull the waxed paper away by about 8–10cm at a time, pressing and smoothing your piece as you go, until you get to the bottom of the board.

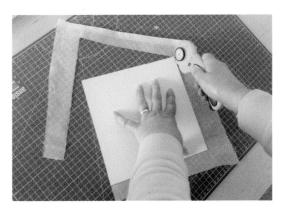

Step 5: Now turn the mounted work over and cut off the excess fabric carefully with a rotary cutter or craft knife.

Your piece is now ready for framing.

Placing the matt onto the piece, which is now mounted and ready for framing.

Step-by-step guide to mounting rough-edged artwork

Equipment
To mount your piece of rough-edged textile art yourself you will need the following equipment:

- A pair of scissors or snips.
- A pencil.
- pH-neutral double-sided tape.
- pH-neutral single-sided tape.
- A needle.
- A small nail and a hammer.
- Thread – either invisible thread or a colour that is compatible with your piece of art.
- A piece of mount board cut slightly larger than your piece of work.

The mount board should be rigid enough to provide stability and support for your piece. I would suggest using a board cut large enough to produce a suitable border all the way around. (For my piece, I have cut the board to give a border of 8cm.)

Preparing and mounting your work
As with the standard mounting technique, it is important to prepare your work correctly, so you get the desired result when it is mounted and framed.

Equipment and materials for mounting a rough-edged piece.

Step 1: Check over your work on both the front and the back for loose threads and remove any that you find. Ensure that the edges are intentionally left in a raw, frayed, or unfinished state. You can enhance this by gently pulling or manipulating the edges to create a textured, fringed look.

Step 2: Place your backing board onto a table and offer up your piece so it is centrally positioned on your mounting board.

Step 3: Use a pencil to mark the position of your piece on the mountboard. Make sure all the marks will be hidden beneath your piece once it is mounted.

Step 4: Now, place the board onto a protective surface, then use a small nail and a hammer to punch some holes through the board at regular intervals along the edge of where your piece will be positioned. You will need to use your judgement as to the best location for the holes if your piece is an irregular shape.

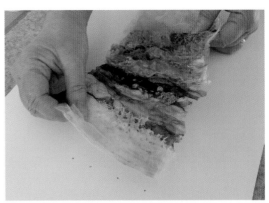

Step 5: Now attach a few strips of the pH-neutral double-sided tape horizontally to the back of your work. How many pieces you need will depend on how large and heavy the piece is. Make sure the strips are evenly spaced and won't be visible once the piece is secured in place.

Step 6: Pull off the backing from the double-sided tape on your work and carefully place your piece in the position you have previously marked on your backing board. When you are happy with the position, apply pressure gently over the areas where the double-sided tape is located to make sure that the piece is secure. Be careful to work around any fragile elements in your work, such as shells.

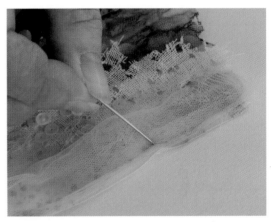

Step 7: Now thread up your needle with your chosen thread and tie a couple of knots in the end. Beginning at the top of the piece, bring the needle through from the back of your board and pull the thread through until it is stopped by the knots, then further secure the thread at the back using a piece of single-sided pH-neutral adhesive tape.

Step 8: Return the needle back through the fabric near to where it came through. Then find the same hole in the backing board and stitch through to the back. Repeat this process for all the holes you have made in the board.

Step 9: Once you have finished, cast off the thread on the back and secure the end with pH-neutral tape, as you did for the start, to prevent the stitches from coming loose over time.

Here you can see the finished, mounted piece, ready for framing.

If you are going to frame your piece without glass, I would suggest you consider applying a clear sealant to protect the piece, paying particular attention to the frayed edges. Several clear matt varnishes on the market will do the job. This will provide some durability. If on the other hand you intend to mount your piece behind glass, as I do, then all that remains is to pop it in your chosen frame. I would advise using a box frame so that your artwork doesn't touch the glass.

FRAMING OPTIONS

Professional framing

Professional framers have a huge amount of experience in framing all sorts of things and will be able to guide you in choosing a suitable colour and size of frame moulding, the matt (mount) and glass that will enhance your textile art piece. They can, of course, mount your work too, but mounting it yourself will keep the cost down.

Although the style and colour of the moulding used to construct the frame can make a huge difference to how the finished piece looks, the glass in your picture frame is perhaps the most important element as it is the medium through which you view your artwork. It is also the component of the frame that will protect your art from dirt, dust and damaging UV light. Below are some options for glazing that I think you should consider although other options, both less and more expensive, are available.

- Plain (standard) glass is inexpensive and reliable. It is usually between 2mm and 3mm in thickness and is suitable for many types of framing work. However, it is reflective and gives very little UV protection.
- Non-reflective glass is also relatively inexpensive, it has a matt surface produced by light etching that diffuses and breaks up reflections. It can sometimes blur the artwork slightly and gives little UV protection.
- Anti-reflective Art Glass AR70 lets the true colours and textures of your artwork shine through. It's coated to eliminate reflections and at the same time gives over 70 per cent protection against UV light. This is my preferred option, but it does cost a little more.

Once you have made your choices you can leave your piece with the framer who will let you know how long they need to get it ready for you.

Buying an off-the-peg frame

This is a more affordable option for many people. However, if you are going to go down this route, I would suggest that you purchase the frame before creating your artwork. That way you can use the mount as described in Chapters 5 and 6 when creating your piece, and you won't have the problem of not being able to find a suitable size frame once you have finished.

When purchasing an off-the-peg frame, please be aware that some come with Perspex®

glazing instead of glass, so double-check the listing description before ordering if you have a preference.

I would suggest choosing a box frame as this will keep your piece well away from the glass/Perspex®, regardless of whether it has any protruding elements. If you decide you don't want your work behind glass or Perspex®, then simply buy an ordinary frame and remove the glazing.

I would personally recommend choosing a simple frame that enhances your artwork without overpowering it. The key is to ensure that the artwork takes centre stage, with the frame serving to complement and accentuate the piece rather than drawing attention away from it. The frame's purpose is to provide a polished finishing touch to your artwork, enriching its overall presentation without diminishing the art itself.

DISPLAYING YOUR ARTWORK

Once your piece is framed you will need to think about where you are going to display it and, in addition to where it will look the best, there are a few things to consider that are specific to textiles when making your decision.

- It is not a good idea to hang textile art where it is going to be exposed to strong sunlight, even if it has been framed behind art glass. As a general guide, you should treat a textile artwork in the same way you would an original watercolour, and I would certainly recommend that you don't hang your work in a conservatory or opposite any window through which the sun can shine directly onto the artwork.
- Even if it is mounted behind glass, textile art is still susceptible to mould if hung in a very damp atmosphere. No frame can be fully hermetically sealed, so avoid the temptation of hanging your seascape in areas of high humidity such as the bathroom or shower room.

MANUFACTURERS AND SUPPLIERS

Sewing machines
https://janome.co.uk

Sewing machine needles
www.schmetz.com

Beading needles
https://www.jjneedles.com

Beads
https://www.spellboundbead.co.uk

General sewing tools and haberdashery
https://www.cottonpatch.co.uk/index.html

Machine and hand threads
https://www.barnyarns.co.uk/en

Fine firm tarlatan scrim backing fabric
https://www.etsy.com/uk/shop/
AlisonWhateleyDesign

Mulberry bark
https://www.stef-francis.co.uk

Mini steam iron
https://www.barnyarns.co.uk/en

Mini heat gun
US https://www.amazon.com UK https://www.
amazon.co.uk

Heat-erasable pens
https://www.pilot-frixion.uk/uk

Adhesive mount board, mounts and frames
https://www.bramptonframing.com

INDEX

colour and texture
  choose weights and textures of
    fabric 44
  colour theory and wheel 43–44
  manipulation techniques
    embellishing machine 46
    heat gun, precautions 46–47
  selecting a colour palette 41
  sheer fabrics
    fine coloured net 45
    organza 44–45
composition, elements of
  colour 37
  depth 37–39
  form and placement
    aspect ratio 32
    implied triangle 32
    Morning Haze 32–34
    rule of thirds 33
    shape and size 32
    sizing mat (or mount) 31
    Solo 35–37
    tension and balance 32
    visiting art galleries 33
  on larger scale 57–63
cutting mat 12
cutting tools
  quick-unpick 12
  rotary cutter 12
  scissors
    embroidery scissors 12
    fabric scissors 12

Embellisher, *see* needle-felting
  machine

hand embroidery stitches
  adding mixed media items 79
    using metal nails and stitching,
      fence representation 79–81
  bullion knot technique 74–75
  buttons, beads and sequins 76
  French knot technique 72–73
  using beachcombing finds
    cleaning beach finds 78
    local regulations 77
  using rusty metal 78–79

inspiration, source of
  in books 21

finished artwork 25–29
magazines 21
sourcing materials
  charity shops 25
  craft stores 25
  online fabric retailers 23
  traditional fabric shops 23
  visiting the coast 17–21
  visual social media platforms
    free stock image websites 22
    Instagram 22
    Pinterest 22
  work of other artists 23

mounting and framing your artwork
  display, things to consider 93
  framing textile art behind
    glass 83
  professional framing 92–93
  purchasing an off-the-peg
    frame 93
  rough-edge mounting of textile
    art 83
    equipment and materials for 89
    step-by-step instructions
      90–91
  standard mounting of
    textile art 83
    equipment and material 84
    step-by-step instructions
      84–88

needle-felting machine 46
needles
  beading needles 14
  hand needles 14
  machine needle
    embroidery needles 13
    metallic needles 14
    sizes 13
    universal needles 13

rules of composition 31

semi-abstract seascape 65–69
sewing machine
  darning or free-motion foot
    10, 11
  styles of 11
  requirement for 9

service recommendations 9
  setting up 10
simple seascape design
  adding headland 50
  area of sand 51
  bleached mulberry bark, to add
    waves 53
  coloured net for sky 53
  fabric adhesive 51
  fabric collection 50
  fabric scraps in foliage colours 53
  heat-erasable pen , outline
    using 50
  impression of grasses, loose-
    weave fabric 54
  patterned fabric 51
  photograph of the layout 54
  requirements for 49
  stitching, free-motion
    embroidery 52
  strips of organza 52

threads
  hand embroidery threads 13
  machine threads
    bobbin thread 12
    top thread 12
tools and equipment
  cutting mat 12
  cutting tools
    quick-unpick 12
    rotary cutter 12
    scissors 11–12
  fabrics
    decorative fabrics 14–15
    Fine Firm Tarlatan Scrim 14
  hand embroidery threads 13
  heat-erasable pens 15
  machine threads 12
  needles
    beading needles 14
    hand needles 14
    machine needle 13–14
  pencils and paper 15
  sewing machine 10
  steam iron and ironing board 15
  temporary fabric adhesives 15
  water-soluble and air-erasable
    pens 15
  working mats 15

First published in 2024 by
The Crowood Press Ltd
Ramsbury, Marlborough
Wiltshire SN8 2HR

enquiries@crowood.com
www.crowood.com

British Library Cataloguing-in-Publication Data

A catalogue record for this book is available from
the British Library.

ISBN 978 0 7198 4432 4
Cover design by Sergey Tsvetkov
Cover image, frontispiece and Contents:
Southgate Studios

Picture Credits
All photographs and illustrations by Philip
Whateley, except where individually credited
otherwise.

The designs in this book are copyright and must
not be stitched for resale. All designs by Alison
Whateley.

Disclaimer: The author and publisher have made
every effort to ensure that all the instructions in the
book are accurate and safe, and therefore cannot
accept liability for any resulting injury, damage or
loss to persons or property, however it may arise.

Typeset by SJmagic DESIGN SERVICES, India
Printed and bound in India by Parksons Graphics

DEDICATION

I would like to thank my husband Phil for
all his love, encouragement and support
during the writing of this book. From your
photographic skills to your command of the
English language and your infinite amount of
patience, I couldn't have done it without you.